CELEBRATING 40 YEAF
ALBUQUERQUE INTERNATIONAI

The World Comes to Albuquerque

published by Rio Grande Books
in collaboration with The Albuquerque International Balloon Fiesta®

CELEBRATING 40 YEARS OF THE
ALBUQUERQUE INTERNATIONAL BALLOON FIESTA®

The World Comes to Albuquerque

Kim Vesely, Dick Brown,
Tom McConnell, & Paul Rhetts, editors

Printed in China
Book design by Paul Rhetts

Library of Congress Cataloging-in-Publication Data

The world comes to Albuquerque : the dream takes flight celebrating 40 years of the Albuquerque international balloon fiesta / Kim Vesely, Dick Brown, Tom McConnell, Paul Rhetts.
p. cm.
ISBN 978-1-890689-97-1 (pbk. : alk. paper)
ISBN 978-1-890689-76-6 (hardcover : alk. paper)
1. Albuquerque International Balloon Fiesta (1976-1990)--History. 2. Albuquerque International Balloon Fiesta (2002-)--History. 3. Ballooning--New Mexico--Albuquerque--History. I. Vesely, Kim, 1954- II. Brown, Dick, 1941- III. McConnell, Tom, 1935- IV. Rhetts, Paul, 1946
 GV762.U5W67 2011
 797.5'109789--dc22
                                                          2010052016

Dedicated to

Richard Abruzzo (1963-2010)
&
Carol Rymer Davis (1944-2010)

Contents

Foreword

Ballooning is an art and a sport of the spontaneous and unexpected. A balloon goes where the wind goes. If the wind changes, as a pilot there isn't much you can do about it except alter your flight plan and tell your chase crew you've changed your mind (again!) about where you're going to land.

What is the *Box*?

Pilots from around the world delight in Albuquerque's fall weather and take advantage of the "box"—a combination of upper and lower level winds that are common in Albuquerque. At different levels the winds go in different directions, meaning that pilots can catch a wind in one direction and then go in another direction by changing altitude. Sometimes they can make the complete "box," ending up landing close to their original take-off place. Part of the enjoyment is never knowing in advance where these gorgeous balloons will fly.

Like ballooning, life takes one down unexpected paths. It is not the type of thing where when you're in second grade and the teacher asks what you want to be when you grow up, you lisp, "I want to be a balloonist!" (There are a few exceptions: Troy Bradley and family come to mind.) So how is it that a former submariner and engineer, a retired professor of pathology, a former TV producer and journalist turned public school information officer, and a former public school information officer turned award-winning book publisher stumbled their way into ballooning—much less writing a book about it?

Millions of people have seen balloons and attended events like the Albuquerque International Balloon Fiesta. They think it's beautiful and fun and they go home. But for some, as George Hahn once described it, "It's like the first time you fall in love." That Pied Piper quality balloons have simply grabs hold and doesn't let go. Before they know it, they're addicted. There's a saying among balloonists: "The first ride is free, the second is $30,000." We can all personally tell you it's true. Sid Cutter famously said, "I know there's money in balloon-

ing. I put it there." We can all personally tell you it's true.

From there, it wasn't that much of a leap for this volume's editors, whose careers all involved professional or techical writing, to migrate towards writing about their ballooning experiences for various publications including *Ballooning* (Dick is a former editor), *Balloon Life*, the local balloon club newsletter *Cloudbouncer*, and the Balloon Fiesta official program. Over the years, their efforts spawned an increasingly urgent series of conversations to the effect of, "When are you going to write your book? You really need to do it before the cast of characters goes off to their great rewards," (which they've been doing with alarming frequency).

One day, we had one of those "duh!" moments. If we took the articles we and others had written for the Balloon Fiesta program throughout the event's history and compiled them, we already had a book! Well, as we were soon to learn, sort of. The intrepid co-editor Paul Rhetts was soon to teach the rest of us how little we really knew about turning a mass of material into a coherent and entertaining whole.

The editors are part of a larger group, the Albuquerque International Balloon Fiesta Heritage Committee, founded by Tom McConnell in 1999 and dedicated to documenting and preserving the Balloon Fiesta's history. The members of the Heritage Committee played an active and enthusiastic role in the development of this project. The Balloon Fiesta Board of Directors—volunteers all—sanctioned *The World Comes to Albuquerque: The Dream Takes Flight* as the official commemorative book for the 40th Balloon Fiesta.

This book is a compilation of material published over a 39-year span documenting in words and pictures the series of events that turned the Balloon Fiesta into one of the country's truly great annual community festivals. Such a compilation, produced as it is from previously written material, has its limitations. Repetitions of important happenings abound, sometimes appearing in 4 or 5 articles. It isn't possible to include 40 years worth of material in a modestly-sized single volume. Invariably, some areas are given short shrift, in particular those not well covered in the original source material. On the other hand, some ancedotes are recounted more than once in articles that originally appeared in different years. In the end, we had some tough choices to make about what we should include to create a book that would be of interest both to those who have never seen a balloon and the committed balloonatic and Balloon Fiesta-goer.

The plus side is that much of the material in this book consists of eyewitness accounts. The authors in many cases lived the events and stories in the book. For each of us, the Balloon Fiesta was a life-changing experience, introducing us to a world of brilliant color, incredible vistas, high adventure, and fascinating people. It also introduced us to

the culture of ballooning, which is based in large measure on sharing the experience with others. We hope that in documenting the development of a world-class event that changed a city and a state, we have also succeeded in sharing with you the delight and wonder we feel every year as balloons ascend into the cool clear Albuquerque skies.

Wishing you fair skies and soft landings,

The editors and members of the Albuquerque International Balloon Fiesta Heritage Committee, 2011

Introduction
Our 40th—Who'da Thunk It?

Lots of folks have asked me when I started the Albuquerque International Balloon Fiesta, did I ever envision it would evolve into the World Class Event that it has. Well duh! Of course not, but as it began to grow it was obvious that there was a next step, or challenge, of sorts.

I was a sort of Chamber of Commerce guy and when we were surprised by the first public turnout (about 20,000 moms, pops, dogs, grandparents on a Saturday morning, and oh yes, only one cop on horseback) with just one radio/television station advertising it, I knew we had a winner! Albuquerque had been looking for a festival and after trying chili cook offs and Mariachi band competitions, these hot air balloons seemed to appeal to ALL the demographics.

I do regret my overzealousness since the event seemed like such a super endeavor, but when you expand to the second year from 13 balloons in April, 1972 to 121 in February, 1973 while hosting the First World Hot Air Balloon Championships, one forgets how the finances will play out. Talk 'bout dumb! I then went to over 100 balloons the third year (1974). Since I was now broke and borrowed to the hilt, luckily our Mayor Harry Kinney stepped in to help. Kinney asked the Chamber of Commerce, the new Albuquerque Convention and Visitors Bureau, the Albuquerque National Bank, the Federal Aviation Agency and private citizens to help. But it was clear that we could not put on the show in February. So I asked the Albuquerque Aerostat Ascension Association, the local club I started in 1972, to hold a rally in February, 1975. They did.

A born optimist, I then bid and captured the Second World Hot Air Balloon Championships, flying 132 balloons in October, 1975. That was the 4th Fiesta.

Again Harry Kinney came to my rescue and by his arm-twisting, a nonprofit citizens committee was set up to take over the Balloon Fiesta. In late 1975 and early 1976, the non-profit corporation Albuquerque International Balloon Fiesta, Inc. was formed.

This is where it developed into a world class event. The Committee had real talent to see the

trees in a forest. Their ideas created a real entertaining and well run event. The Balloon Glows, the Key Grabs, the Concession Row, The Gondola Club, Park and Ride, The Discovery Center, The Special Shapes, Premium Fireworks, American Challenge Gas Balloon Race, Corporate Village, Albuquerque Aloft where 100s of balloons lift off all over the city at the same time (I wanted to name it the Balloon Explosion but got overruled). There are many other attractions, but I should mention our medical response facilities and our security system are second to none.

One story I remember from the 1973 Fiesta: During the 1st World Championships, which was held at the fairgrounds, I had promised the FAA that we would not interfere with the air traffic. Wouldn't you know, the very first flight went directly south not only over the Albuquerque air-

port but also Sandia Base and Manzano Base where the Nukes are stored. Boy, I knew I was in trouble. The bases locked down and the airport manager, who was my aviation business landlord and a friend, was able to settle down the tower personnel to be co-operative. The Bases shut down for the rest of the week. Talk about dodging the bullet! Anyway, that event hit all the news and television media and made Albuquerque the Balloon Capital of the World!

There are 1000's of volunteers without whom this Fiesta could not happen— from the launch directors (Zebras) to scorers to parking to admissions all of whom take a professional attitude toward their jobs. I consider myself to be one of them and am quite proud to work with these folks. It has been an honor and privilege to have been a part of the Albuquerque International Balloon Fiesta for these forty years.

Sid Cutter
Albuquerque, NM
April 23, 2010

So How Do They Fly?

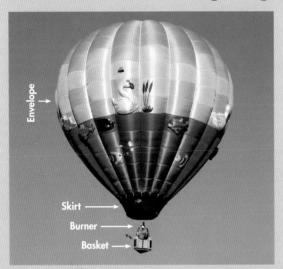

Envelope

Skirt
Burner
Basket

Balloons fly because the atmosphere inside the envelope (the "bag" or fabric part of the balloon) is lighter than the surrounding air—so much lighter that it is strong enough to lift the weight of balloon and passengers. There are two major types of balloons, hot air and gas, and although the mechanics of flying the two are somewhat different, the basic principle applies. Hot air balloons use a powerful burner, suspended between the basket and the envelope, to keep the air hot to gain lift. The burner is fueled by liquid propane carried in tanks in the basket. Gas balloons use a rather different method to stay aloft. The envelopes of gas balloons are sealed and filled with a "lighter-than-air" gas, such as helium or hydrogen. Gas balloons are controlled by varying the weight of the balloon and therefore carry "ballast" (usually sand or water) that can be dumped overboard to lighten the load. The pilot dumps ballast to go up, and has a valve in the envelope which can be opened to release gas and cause the balloon to descend.

The dream of flight spans millennia, from the time humans watched birds soar aloft and wished they could sprout wings and ascend to the heavens. But when that dream finally came true, there was nary a wing in sight on the first craft that carried men to the skies.

Enlightenment-era thinkers and tinkerers in France, the papermakers Jacques and Étienne Montgolfier, became curious about the fact that scraps of paper were carried aloft in the hot air and smoke of a fire. They built a paper container—a bag, or "envelope"—to see if it could contain the heat and smoke and be carried upward. It did.

As their experimental envelopes became bigger, the Montgolfier brothers attempted successfully to send animals aloft in September 1783 from Versailles, on the same principle twentieth century scientists applied by sending dogs and chimpanzees into space before risking human life. The first passengers—a sheep, a duck, and a rooster—did just fine on that first balloon ride except that the sheep broke the rooster's wing. Not long after, on November 21, 1783, physicist Jean-François Pilâtre de Rozier and army major Marquis François d'Arlandes, completed the first successful hot-air balloon flight from the Bois de Boulogne in western Paris. Days later, Professor J.A.C. Charles, who had been do-ing similar experiments to the Montgolfiers' but using hydrogen as a lifting gas, ascended from the Tuilières Gardens in Paris in the first gas balloon.

The first balloon flights created the same excitement later generations would know with the dawning of powered flight at the beginning of the twentieth century and the race to the moon in the 1960s. The daring men, and a few women, brave enough to step into a balloon basket and leave terra firma were regarded as heroes, and many barnstormed the county fair circuits performing "spectacular feats of stratospheric skill" like those of the fictional Wizard of L. Frank Baum's The Wizard of Oz. As the Wizard told Dorothy and her companions in the 1939 film when asked, "Were you frightened?": "You are talking to a man who has laughed in the face of death, sneered at doom, and chuckled at catastrophe. I was petrified!"*

It was in that tradition that the first balloon came to Albuquerque, nearly 90 years before the first Albuquerque International Balloon Fiesta.

*The Wizard of Oz, screenplay by Noel Langley, Florence Ryerson, and Edgar Allan Woolf, based on the book by L. Frank Baum.

Inflation of Van Tassel's balloon on Second Street, between Railroad (Central) and Gold, at the site of the present-day Sunshine Building. Photographs courtesy of the William F. Stamm family.

Albuquerque's Early Ballooning Heritage

"A balloon ascension invariably leaves a strong, lasting and vivid impression on the mind and memory. It attracts all classes, old and young, all tastes and interests, for a balloon ascension is at all times a novel and sublime sight, exhibiting, as it does, man's dominion over the very air he breathes. As a spectacle, it fixes the attention of every beholder." – *Albuquerque Morning Journal*, June 17, 1882

13

Joseph Blondin (left) and Roy Stamm (right) pose as the hydrogen gas generator fills the balloon.

Let us step back in time to 1882, two years after the Santa Fe Railroad arrived in Albuquerque. It was the year when the first wagon bridge was constructed across the Rio Grande at Albuquerque, a 1600-foot wooden span costing $22,000. With the railroad came phenomenal growth. New Town had been laid out on the east and west sides of the tracks, and the principal roadway had been named Railroad Avenue (now Central), because it had tracks set into the roadbed from the Santa Fe Depot in New Town to the Plaza in Old Town. A ride on the mule-drawn streetcar cost three cents. It is said that the cost of living was a "trifle higher than back East." House rentals varied from $12 to $40 per month. City laborers earned $2 a day while carpenters and stonecutters, in great demand by the railroad, earned as much as $4.50 a day.

Albuquerque Box Debuts at First Balloon Event

Professor Park Van Tassel, a native of New York, owned the Elite Saloon. He was also an experienced aeronaut with a balloon on order from Professor F.F. Martin in San Francisco, one of the most celebrated aeronauts on the Pacific coast. He paid $850 for the balloon and shipping. It was 38 feet in diameter, 30,000 cubic feet in volume, and designed to carry two-thirds of a ton. It included grapnel hook, anchor and basket. Among the paraphernalia was the latest in barometers from London, an instrument highly prized by all professional aeronauts of the time.

By June 18th, it was decided that the first Albuquerque balloon ascension should take place on the Fourth of July holiday. "Albuquerque is to have an attraction that will throw everything else into the shade. A picnic or a parade may be found almost any time or anywhere, but the ascension of a real balloon, carrying real live passengers, is something that has never been witnessed in New Mexico, and is a rarity in any part of the country. To have the pleasure of such a sight as this will well repay the people of other parts of the (NM) territory for the trouble and expense of a trip to Albuquerque."

For the next two weeks, the *Journal* advertised that the balloon "City of Albuquerque" would ascend on Tuesday, July 4th. "Prof. Van Tassel will superintend the inflation and make the perilous ascent, accompanied by a reporter of the *Journal*, who agrees to give a full and correct report of their experience while 'up in a balloon.' By all means witness the thrilling and exciting sensation as the aeronaut takes his place in the frail basket; the perilous start and the noble and sublime scene of the great ascent up among the clouds."

On July 2nd, the *Journal* reported "Newspapers in all parts of the territory have made favorable mention of the attractions to be offered at Albuquerque on the Fourth—especially the balloon ascension – and since the railroads have advertised to carry visitors at half-fare, the prospect is good for an immense crowd. Prof. Van Tassel has all his arrangements completed. His balloon is all ready for the voyage, and those who come to Albuquerque will have the pleasure of witnessing the first ascension ever made in New Mexico."

All through the day on July 3rd, Albuquerque's gas works superintendent was engaged in manufacturing coal gas for the inflation of the balloon. Sometimes called illuminating gas because it was commonly used for indoor lighting, coal gas is a mixture of hydrogen, methane and carbon dioxide. It is produced by burning coal in a low oxygen environment. Inflation began at 5:00 pm with the hope that the ascension could take place between the hours of 10:00 am and noon on the Fourth. There was a parade to the Fairgrounds near Old Town, music by the city band, burro races, sack races, wheelbarrow races with blind-folded contestants, firecrackers, and a baseball game between the Albuquerque Browns and a mysterious hand-picked nine from the Opera House. People flocked from all directions, arriving by wagon, on horseback and on foot. Stars and stripes hung from poles and saloon men did a great business.

The crowd gathered on Second Street, between Railroad and Gold avenues in New Town, to witness the inflation of Van Tassel's balloon. But the balloon filled too slowly to satisfy the impatient crowd. "As the hour advertised for the ascension came and passed and there was still no sign of the aeronaut starting on his journey, the people became restless and a general buzz of dissatisfaction could be heard." Disgruntled, the crowd moved down Railroad Avenue to the Fairgrounds to see the races

Blondin, Stamm, and spectators pose for pictures just prior to lift-off.

and other sports that had been planned. For the next two hours, every streetcar was filled to capacity as the crowd vacated the launch site.

"Shortly after 5 o'clock word was telephoned to Old Town that the balloon would start on its aerial flight at 6:15 precisely. This announcement was made from the grandstand and the crowd again started for New Town." Just as buses transport spec-

The balloon drifts northwest toward the two-story historic John Pearce House that still stands at 718 Central Avenue.

tators to today's Balloon Fiesta, Albuquerque's first "fiesta" patrons reboarded the streetcars and journeyed back to the launch site. "Although the balloon was scarcely two-thirds full, Prof. Van Tassel decided to risk the trip rather than disappoint the people who had waited so long to witness the ascension. At the appointed time everything was in readi-

ness and the bold navigator of the air stepped into the basket. It was found that the "City of Albuquerque" would not carry her captain with more than 45 pounds of sand ballast, let alone any passengers, so she was turned loose with only him on board."

Just as the balloon started on its maiden flight, Van Tassel emptied a bag of sand over the side, most of which hit the head of a spectator who later sued for damages.

"The balloon rose high up above the house tops and moved slowly to the south, when it appeared to stop its lateral motion, and went straight up among the clouds. Another current of air was struck and the ship took a northwesterly direction." This wind shift phenomenon would later be known as the famous Albuquerque Box.

"The course of the balloon was closely watched by the thousands who were on the streets. It gradually diminished in size, as it rose higher and higher until the basket in which the professor was riding looked no larger than a derby hat. When it had reached a point directly over Old Town, the airship commenced to descend and land safely in a corn field in the rear of the Fairgrounds. As soon as it was seen just where Prof. Van Tassel would alight, quite a number of men started for the place on horseback, and a Journal scribe obtained a conveyance in which to bring back the aeronaut and his balloon.

"The professor was found, none the worse for his voyage, busily engaged in emptying the balloon of the gas. This was soon accomplished and the party with the airship safely loaded started for New Town, arriving at the starting point at 9 o'clock.

"A grand ovation was awaiting the party at the Elite Saloon and many and loud were the expressions of congratulations with which Van Tassel was greeted. All united in saying that the ascension was a success in every sense of the word."

Another newspaper, the *Evening Review*, interviewed Van Tassel after the flight. At the west end of Old Town, high above the river, Van Tassel told the reporter "I thought I would go up higher, and emptied the contents of one bag of ballast over the side, and in a few moments the barometer registered 14,207 feet."

Van Tassel's Misadventure at 1882 New Mexico Territorial Fair

Immediately following Van Tassel's history-making balloon ascension, the executive committee of the Fair Association initiated negotiations with the Professor to make another ascension. By July 8th, the *Journal* was promoting the next balloon event during the Second Annual New Mexico Territorial Fair scheduled to begin on September 18, 1882. "The great balloon ascension will take place on the fourth day of the Fair, and will assist in attracting thousands of visitors." It is interesting to note that our early Balloon Fiestas took place at the NM State Fairgrounds, also on Central (Railroad) Avenue.

A few days before the planned ascension, the Journal ran display ads for "One of the Greatest Attractions Ever Presented to the People of New Mexico." The balloon was to be inflated in New Town and towed over to the Fairgrounds near the river. Van Tassel planned to make "captive ascensions in the forenoon and in the afternoon the rope will be cut." Another ad set the launch time as 4:30 pm when the Professor would "make a voyage to the upper world."

Stamm dumps sand ballast as the balloon rises from a vacant lot near Sixth and Central.

On the morning of September 20th, the filling of Van Tassel's balloon was commenced at the corner of Third Street and Gold Avenue but was not completed until noon the next day. It was then secured with a rope and towed by 100 men to the Fairgrounds. Unfortunately, "the rope holding the balloon parted, and while a number of those close by attempted to hold the ponderous ship, it rose quickly toward the clouds. Without a hand to control and guide its velocity, the ascending gas bag quickly reached an altitude of a mile…" The balloon soared directly above the Fairgrounds and

17

More altitude is needed quickly as the balloon closes in on near-field obstructions.

burst. The "torn shreds acted like an immense parachute" and "the unruly monster floated off to the north." It fell to the ground about a quarter mile from where it started and several parties hauled it back by wagon, and so ended Van Tassel's balloon escapades in Albuquerque.

Balloon Fiesta or Balloon Fiasco?

Albuquerque's next ballooning experience was Prof. Thomas Scott Baldwin's ascension during the 1889 New Mexico Territorial Fair. Taking advantage of the special event, Albuquerque saloonkeepers hiked the price of a glass of beer from 5 cents to 10 cents.

Prof. Baldwin made his first balloon ascension in 1875 and spent the next 10 years perfecting balloon ascensions at shows and fairs. In 1885, to spice up his performance, he made one of the very first parachute jumps from a balloon. Two years later, he invented the first folding parachute and by the time he had been invited to New Mexico's Fair, he had become one of the highest paid parachute exhibitionists in the country.

His first balloon ascension in Albuquerque was scheduled for October 2nd, a time of year that now features the annual Albuquerque International Balloon Fiesta. Unfortunately, the Professor could not get his balloon inflated properly and so he could not launch. The pioneer aviator explained that he forgot to take into consideration Albuquerque's rarified air and promised to do better the next day.

On his next attempt, Prof. Baldwin managed a proper inflation. Several hundred men held down the balloon until the professor arrived. He looked at his balloon and exclaimed, "Oh, ain't she a dandy. Who says we ain't going high this time?" He then attached himself to the balloon with some ropes and shouted "Let her go!"

As the balloon began to rise, the ropes broke and the professor dropped to the ground, landing unceremoniously on his posterior, and the balloon went off without him.

Things went better during Prof. Baldwin's third attempt. On the final day of the Fair, he soared to 3000 feet and redeemed himself in the eyes of the public.

Later in California, Albuquerque's first aeronauts, Professors Baldwin and Van Tassel, went into partnership performing balloon-parachute demonstrations all over the world. Baldwin had a distinguished career developing airships and airplanes for the Army and Navy. He died in 1923 and was buried in Arlington National Cemetery with full military honors. Van Tassel, his wife and family all gained notoriety making daredevil parachute jumps from balloons. One of his jumps in Hawaii went terribly wrong and he dropped into the Pacific, two miles from shore. News reports said that the sharks got him but in reality, the sharks got his partner, Joe Lawrence of Albuquerque, who was substituting for Van Tassel on the ill-fated flight. Van Tassel died in Oakland, California in 1931.

Professor Elmo also had his share of troubles. On September 18, 1890, after several attempts, he succeeded in raising his smoke balloon for a parachute jump, only to have it collapse at 200 feet. He miraculously escaped serious injury and later explained his mishap to a reporter: "In digging our furnace we encountered surface water at a depth of about 14 inches, and as this water was constantly creeping in from all sides it was impossible to keep the furnace from making steam, which soon filled the balloon and gave it the appearance of being well filled, when in reality it could hardly support its own weight."

Nine years later, at the 1899 New Mexico Territorial Fair, Professor Zeno had a little trouble with his balloon. On the opening day the balloonist became tangled in the ropes and the parachute he was wearing opened as he was leaving the ground. He reportedly made a successful "illuminated" ascension that night, perhaps an unwitting precursor to Albuquerque's famous Balloon Glow.

Albuquerque's earliest balloonists were showmen and some were unrivaled in aviation history. It was probably inevitable that Albuquerque would one day become the Balloon Capital of the World.

The balloon barely clears an electric wire of the Central Avenue trolley.

Ballooning Success at 1907 New Mexico Territorial Fair

Roy Stamm, a local fruit wholesaler, was appointed Secretary of the Fair Association in 1907. Joseph Blondin, an experienced balloonist and former Albuquerque resident, had sold Stamm and his associates on a plan to use a captive hydrogen balloon at the 27th Annual Territorial Fair scheduled for October 7-12.

Blondin was born in Chicago in 1879. He was first exposed to ballooning in 1896 while study-

19

Shortly after this photo was taken, the balloon veered southeast towards the mountains.

ing music in Paris. He had clerked for the Santa Fe Railroad in Albuquerque and prospected in the Jemez Mountains, and in 1904 left Albuquerque for the World's Fair in St. Louis. There he worked with Prof. Baldwin who by then had become famous by flying America's first successful powered airship, the California Arrow. Again bitten by the balloon

bug, Blondin went to work at a New York balloon factory owned by A. Leo Stevens. He performed balloon ascensions in the East and became a charter member of the Aero Club of America that later became the National Aeronautics Association. In 1907, Blondin bought a 25,000 cubic foot balloon and returned to Albuquerque as Stevens' western sales agent.

Blondin converted a street sprinkling wagon to a hydrogen gas generator; however, numerous leaks made it impossible to fill the balloon. On the last day of the 1907 Fair, a company of 25 cavalrymen from Fort Wingate walked the one-third filled bag two miles through the South Valley to the city gas plant where the inflation was to be completed with coal gas. It was Friday, October 11th. The balloon was anchored with sandbags at the plant and its inflation valve was coupled to the gas system. By 10:00 am the next day, the bag appeared full. The balloon was walked back downtown to the Fairgrounds.

Blondin was quoted as saying, "I admit that the sporting element in ballooning is great and that this is what attracts many to the profession. Right here in Albuquerque, though I have been here but a few days, a dozen young men have asked to be allowed to accompany me on my flight."

Unfortunately, the balloon was not sufficiently buoyant to lift ballast and balloonist, let alone passengers. Late that day, Blondin flew solo up the Rio Grande Valley, and drifted 18 miles until the evening air cooled the gas bag. Over Alameda, he was shot at eight times, but suffered no damage. On landing, he stood on the load ring and hung on to the shrouds to lessen the shock from impact on the mesa west of Corrales, an area where, in the early

1970s, modern sport ballooning in Albuquerque really got its start. After the Fair, Blondin sold his balloon to Stamm and went back to prospecting. Stamm kept the gas bag packed away during the 1908 Fair.

President Sees Balloon at 1909 New Mexico Territorial Fair

For the 29th Annual New Mexico Territorial Fair, the Fair Association had contracted with the Strobel Airship Company for a special attraction. The company specialized in barnstorming shows with small cigar-shaped dirigible balloons powered by a man pedaling a suspended bicycle-like mechanism to turn a propeller. Throughout the West, the Fair had advertised the simultaneous appearance of President William Howard Taft and the Strobel flying machines.

Just prior to leaving for Albuquerque, the only Strobel airship capable of lifting at Albuquerque's mile-high altitude, crashed and burned in Mexico City. Half the western population was coming to Albuquerque. Fortunately, Joseph Blondin had been conferring with fair officials earlier that summer about operating a captive balloon at the Fair. He also planned a long flight after the Fair in which he hoped to arrive in St. Louis in time for the annual Gordon Bennett balloon race, the recently resurrected classic gas balloon distance race that Albuquerque hosted in the 1990s. In bragging to the Fair Association and the press about the safety record of gas balloons, Blondin explained that smoke ballooning was unsafe, and that the list of accidents and deaths resulting from this form of ballooning and associated parachute stunts was appalling.

With time running short and no Strobel airship on its way, Blondin, Stamm and a 10-man crew quickly set to work on their own balloon show. They wrestled with a wooden tank generator for the hydrogen production at the Territorial Fairgrounds.

One night at 3:30 am, the gas showed signs of lifting the water-seal, a large inverted washtub on top of the generator. Stamm rushed to the rescue by throwing himself over the tub in a desperate attempt to hold down the gas. Instantly, the tub, Stamm and a geyser of sulfuric acid shot several feet in the air—his first ascension. Stamm had accidentally mixed water with acid instead of the reverse and succeeded in splattering his clothing and most of the launch site with acid.

As the Fair opened, the wind subsided and after a 30-hour inflation, the bag was filled. Blondin went up first, then Stamm. President Taft on a special train approaching the city saw the balloon tethering over the Fairgrounds. The President congratulated Blondin and Stamm, Albuquerque's honor was saved, and the aerial exhibition was the hit of the 1909 Fair. The first passengers at this early balloon "fiesta" were the ground crew, the soldiers from Fort Wingate, followed by hundreds of men, women and children. For one dollar, they rode 10 minutes on a 500-foot tether. One day, Blondin and two young ladies, while ascending on the tether rope, were hit by a gust of wind. The basket crashed into the roof of a house on Gold Avenue, but there was no damage or injury. Stamm and Blondin decided the show was over for that day.

Pioneering Free Flight Over the Mountains

The Fair Association had advertised that an attempt would be made to break the endurance and distance records for balloon flight. The winds were up again at the close of the Fair, the sulfuric acid supply was exhausted and there was no way of replacing the hydrogen lost during the Fair ascensions. A considerable amount of the provisions and ballast had to be left behind since the bag was only three-quarters full. Ballast is the lifeblood of gas ballooning since dumping compensates for gas loss. Flight control is achieved by discharging ballast to rise, and valving off gas to descend. Sometimes a trail rope is used as recoverable ballast and a grapnel hook can be slid down the line during high wind landings.

On Tuesday, October 19, 1909, at 10:55 am, Stamm and Blondin climbed into the basket. The launch from a vacant lot at the corner of Sixth and Central was observed by Mayor Felix Lester and a large cheering crowd. The basket cleared an electric wire of the Central Avenue trolley by inches as Stamm frantically dumped a whole bag of the precious ballast. The balloon shot up a mile, paused over Albuquerque as if in doubt as to which way to go, then waltzed its way into a 40 mph current. Stamm wrote in his journal: "Sublime is your complete detachment from the sounds and restraints of earth. For the world drops away from all around you; literally and figuratively, you are exalted!"

They cleared the Manzanita Mountains by 1000 feet and from Albuquerque appeared to be a speck on the eastern skyline. On the other side, the warmer air of Estancia Valley caused the balloon to rise to 13,000 feet. The aeronauts were shot at as they passed over Estancia. They seemed to be heading for Vaughn, but then dropped 1700 feet per minute and avoided a crash at the base of the Pedernal Hills by discharging the last bag of ballast and the grapnel hook at 100 feet. Stamm and Blondin landed safely in Torrance County and returned by wagon to Estancia and Kennedy, then by train back to Albuquerque.

Epilogue

After Stamm and Blondin's 90-mile free flight that year, Albuquerque aeronautics gave way to powered flight. Winged contraptions filled the skies where pioneer balloonists like Van Tassel, Baldwin, Elmo, Zeno, Blondin and Stamm once drifted about in their gas-filled aerostats. The first airplane in Albuquerque was brought in by express for the 1910 Territorial Fair and the following year Roy Stamm's brother, Ray, became the first airplane passenger to be carried from our mile-high elevation. Roy Stamm and Joe McCanna were the next passengers to fly in the single engine Curtis biplane.

After Statehood in 1912, New Mexico aviation progressed with the rest of the Nation. Americans were witnessing the evolution of powered flight. Seeing that the airplane would make progress where the balloon could not, Albuquerque balloonist Joe Blondin left the Southwest to work for the "Curtis Flyers," a heavier-than-air flight exhibition team. He later patented several airplane flight control inventions and died in 1951. Roy Stamm, a life-long Albuquerque resident, passed away seven years later. While the greatest chapter in Albuquerque ballooning would not be written about until decades later, the heydays around the turn of the century were the true beginning of "balloon fiestas" in our city. They are as much a part of Albuquerque's ballooning heritage as today's Balloon Fiestas. After 122 years, a balloon ascension still fixes the attention of every beholder and leaves a lasting and vivid impression on the mind and memory.

❏ Dick Brown, 2004

From 1910 to 1972, the airplane was the unchallenged king of flight in Albuquerque. But ballooning in the United States was not completely dead. Several Gordon Bennett distance races were hosted in the eastern U.S; adventurers and scientists like the Piccard brothers made daring manned scientific and even a few pleasure flights. New Mexico's Holloman Air Force Base played a major role in the manned stratospheric balloon flights of the 1950s and 1960s. Perhaps the most famous of those flights was the Excelsior III mission of August 16, 1960. Col. Joe Kittinger jumped from his craft at an altitude of 102,800 feet. As of 2010, his world-record-setting epic free fall from the edge of outer space back into the atmosphere had still not been bested.

Meanwhile others, notably the late Ed Yost, were engaged in other balloon-related research for the military—specifically, the development of a practical hot-air balloon using a propane-fed burner to generate heat in the envelope. The technology did not prove very practical for military uses, but by the early 1960s Yost and others began developing hot-air balloon systems for recreational use. Eventually, a few of these balloons put in appearances in New Mexico. The New Mexico State University student newspaper, the Round Up, noted in a September 22, 1971, article that "astronaut" Charles MacArthur would conduct lectures on the subjects of balloon building, basket building, and piloting, to be followed by an evening balloon ascension. The event was part of a "Festival of Arts" which also included an appearance by philosopher-engineer R. Buckminster Fuller (the geodesic dome inventor).

The revival of ballooning in Albuquerque had arrived just four months earlier as Sid Cutter's act of decorating desperation—but, well, he told the story himself, in a short article included in the press kit for the third Balloon Fiesta in 1974.

26

The Party

I remember my interest not wandering often from airplanes, having grown up in the business—getting my first "official" lessons when I was nine years old, and flying commercially at 18, but then it happened. That was in May 1971, and I was running the business my father began in 1928. We had a good year going. I thought it would be great to throw a party for all our customers and friends over the many years as a sort of thanks and to show off our facilities and capabilities. I wanted this to be a unique party to end all parties (the kind you could only afford to throw every 43 years), doing it up super right with the way you visualize such an affair with ice-carvings, a pig with an apple in its mouth, etc.

This was also about the time Snoopy was reaching a peak in popularity with his flying dog house and his feud with the Red Baron, so I adopted the theme of World War I aviation. Our main hangar is quite large, making conventional decorations seem inadequate, but I had invited some 1500 people (about 2500 showed up) and we needed the room. I set up the movie *Those Magnificent Men In Their Flying Machines* showing continuously on a screen (canvas drop), about 25 feet square, but it only took up one corner of the 44,000 square foot hangar. I set up eight bars and dressed all the bartenders in World War I aviation costumes, had a stage with a German Ompah band, 100' table of foods, a large area to dance, and displayed the full line of Beechcraft airplanes (about 12 models), but the place still looked vacant. I thought I could suspend vintage bi-planes from the beams, but the cost and effort was prohibitive. Then is when it hit me—a balloon as a centerpiece.

This Old Bag For Rent *(a.k.a.* Betsy Ross*): Sid Cutter's first balloon, 1971.*

Party mix: Beechcrafts and Balloons.

"Snoopy" (a.k.a. Sid Cutter), mom Virginia Cutter, and the "Red Baron" (a.k.a. Bill Cutter).

But where and how do I get one of those? I had never seen one or even a picture of one except in *Around the World in 80 Days*. I knew that helium would be too expensive and hydrogen was extremely dangerous, but I heard that some progress had recently been made making hot air balloons practical. I checked around to rent one to inflate inside the hangar as a centerpiece. The owners thought I was nuts, but priced me $800 plus travel with no guarantee it could be done.

That seemed kind of steep and it occurred to me that a balloon of our own might be of good promotional value. Balloons weren't too popular then, and so a manufacturer said he could build us one in ten days, the time left till the party, but couldn't possibly ship it to us in time. I said I'd pick

it up the day before by private airplane if he would show me how to inflate it.

We had a deal! I found out that Tornado Alley was between Albuquerque and Sioux Falls, South Dakota on the day of pick up but the show (party) must go on! We got back to Albuquerque that night late after learning how to inflate it and began decorating the next day—yep!! You guessed it—it wouldn't fit in the hangar. But we stuffed it in between the rafters and the floor. It looked more like a squashed mushroom than a balloon, but everybody understood.

There was a little alcohol and my brother spouting how I was an expert and would launch on its maiden voyage the next morning at 6:30 a.m. Oh, me! I had never seen a balloon until the day before,

Centerfold of the 1973 Balloon Fiesta program showing Sid Cutter's Wile E Coyote® *and the AAAA* Roadrunner *balloons over Albuquerque.*

and was not yet convinced they really flew because my inflation lesson was in the Sioux Falls auditorium. Well, I was in one of those corners where a fellow would rather die than make an ass out of himself, so the stage was set. The party didn't get over until 2:30 a.m., so I wasn't feeling too champion when I was picked up at 5:30 a.m.. At 6:30 a.m., right on schedule, I took my mother up (rope attached) and began to teach myself how to anticipate the balloon and how to fly. It was the only natural thing to do, taking my mother up first because all night before we told everybody we bought the balloon for her birthday and she should be the first to ride in her own balloon. It would have been just fine with me to have her go by herself as I was scared to death.

Up to the end of the 150-foot rope and back down—out goes Mrs. Cutter (to work), and in jumps brother Bill—up to the end of the rope—back down? Hardly! Our smart ground crew untied it and off we slowly drifted—a free balloon with a couple of dumb airplane pilots, both in stark terror.

The rest is history now, with 25 balloons based in Albuquerque, organizer of the First World Hot Air Balloon Championships with 138 balloons and 17 nations participating, organizer of the First Crossing of nine balloons from the Bahama Islands to the Florida coast, and now the Third Albuquerque International Balloon Fiesta—a festival born in a one balloon town only three years ago.

❑ Sid Cutter, 1974

The year was 1972. *The Godfather*, starring Marlon Brando and Al Pacino, won three Oscars, including Best Picture; the TV series, *All in the Family*, with Carroll O'Connor, Jean Stapleton, Sally Struthers and Rob Reiner, was beginning its second year; Richard Nixon was President, and Bruce King was Governor. It was the 50th anniversary of KOB Radio and the 100th anniversary of Jules Verne's lofty balloon adventure novel with Captain Phileas Phogg in *Around the World in Eighty Days*.

And on a cool April morning, 20,000 sleepy spectators gathered at the west side of Coronado Shopping Center to witness Albuquerque's inaugural hot air ballooning event. The crowd exceeded everyone's expectations, including the Police Department that assigned only one mounted patrolman.

But first, let's step back four months—the local balloon club, Albuquerque Aerostat Ascension Association, affectionately known as "Quad A," had just been launched when Maxie Anderson, Jesse Baxter, Don Draper, Jim Doolittle, George Kloepfer, Graham McNary, Eddie Perchak and Al Ratchner met at Sid Cutter's home. The nine charter members had purchased a club balloon called *Roadrunner*, which made its maiden voyage in early January 1972.

Dick McKee, general manager of KOB Radio, approached Sid about flying the *Roadrunner* balloon to help launch festivities for the station's 50th anniversary. He asked: "What is the largest balloon race that's ever been held?"

Sid replied, "Nineteen balloons in England." "Can we get 19 balloons here?"

"I don't know why not."

Albuquerque's first hot air balloon gathering was in 1972 in the Coronado Center parking lot. Quad A's Roadrunner balloon (above) prepares to launch.

Albuquerque's First
Balloon Fiesta

Left to right, Matt Wiederkehr, Carter Twedt and Denny Floden inflate their balloons at Coronado Center.

In an effort to beat the British, Sid scrambled to assemble enough balloons to set a new world record. Balloonists from all across the country were invited to fly in Albuquerque on April 8, 1972. KOB radio and television advertised the event, but the newspapers paid little attention. Twenty-one balloons committed but last minute cancellations and shipping delays due to a late season snowstorm in Chicago, resulted in only thirteen participating balloons. Nevertheless, the First Balloon Fiesta set a record as the largest hot air balloon race in North America.

The centerpiece for the "KOB Birthday Bash & Balloon Race" was the Southwest version of a Hare and Hound race—a Roadrunner-Coyote Race, sanctioned by the Balloon Federation of America (BFA), the national ballooning organization representing the United States in the Federation Aéro-

nautique Internationale (FAI). Don Kersten, BFA President, had just returned from an FAI conference in Paris. He had been asked by the FAI to find a suitable host city for the First World Hot Air Balloon Championships.

Back on the launch field at Coronado, pilots arrived from Arizona, California, Iowa, Michigan, Minnesota, Nevada and Texas. KOB's Tom Rutherford, as the master of ceremonies, used the opportunity to launch his campaign for a seat in the New Mexico State Senate. This accounts for why celebrities Penny Marshall, Slim Pickens and Rob Reiner were on hand as Sid Cutter and Don Draper lifted off in AAAA's *Roadrunner* balloon. KOB TV4's Dr. George Fischbeck was also on-hand as the "official" weatherman. In a short while, the Governor fired the starting pistol and, although the shot could not be heard over the burners, the race was on. As Sid looked back at the 12 "Coyote" balloons in hot pursuit, he remarked, "Well, Don, we have finally seen a balloon race." Among the pack of coyotes was Dennis Floden, otherwise known as Captain Phogg, who the next year would become the world's first Hot Air Balloon Champion. Other pilots included Bill Cutter, Gene Dennis, Don Kersten, Oscar Kratz, Bill Murtorff, Don Piccard, Wilma Piccard, Karl Stefan, Brent Stockwell, Carter Twedt and Matt Wiederkehr.

The flotilla of brightly-colored hot air balloons, most trailing advertising banners, drifted northeast from Coronado. Albuquerqueans were in awe, witnessing hot-air ballooning for the first time. Among them were John and Carol Davis who, right then and there, decided that ballooning was for them. The next day, they rounded up some friends and each contributed to the purchase of a balloon called

Mellow Yellow. Carol reportedly raised her share by selling her Pinto.

The winner of the "First Albuquerque Roadrunner-Coyote Balloon Race" (soon everyone simply referred to the event as the "First Balloon Fiesta") was Don Piccard, landing only 184 feet from the *Roadrunner*. Don's wife, Wilma, in her own balloon, placed second by landing 206 feet away.

Kersten was highly impressed by Albuquerque's southwestern hospitality and urged the city to submit a bid for the First World Hot Air Balloon Championships. Sid and Tom joined forces to establish World Balloon Championships, Inc. They submitted what turned out to be the only bid and—just like that—Albuquerque was selected. In February 1973 the city hosted its second Balloon Fiesta in conjunction with the First World's. Sid's new *Wile E Coyote®* balloon, emblazoned with the Warner Bros. cartoon characters and the words "Albuquerque International Roadrunner-Coyote Fiesta," became the official balloon for the event. For a while, Tom served on Sid's chase crew but he was always getting lost. After waiting in open fields too many times, Sid let him know that he was not much good on the chase crew and—because you cannot steer a balloon anyway—Tom would just have to become a pilot.

World Balloon Championships went on to become World Balloon Corporation, a highly successful commercial balloon company. Sid used to say, "I know there's money in ballooning because I put it there." Tom did indeed become a licensed balloon pilot as well as New Mexico's youngest State Senator. Throughout his 24-year political career, he served as the brunt of numerous jokes about politicians being full of hot air. Sid has enjoyed a 30-year career in ballooning and is widely accepted as the Founder of Hot Air Ballooning in Albuquerque.

On September 28, 1996, at Coronado Center, the First Fiesta was re-enacted with 12 of the 13 balloonists attending. With KOB Radio again calling the play-by-play on the launch field, this special celebration marked the Silver Anniversary of the Albuquerque International Balloon Fiesta.

Who would ever have envisioned that those 13 balloons flying from Coronado would continue as an annual community event for 30 years, an event that has taken on a life of its own, now with over a thousand participating balloons? Maybe only one person could have such a vision—Sid Cutter. No one has done more to give the sport a lift and to land Albuquerque's unique reputation as the ballooning capital of the world.

❏ Dick Brown, 2001

Denny Floden launches, while (left to right) Gene Dennis, Willie Piccard and Don Piccard make final preparations.

35

THE ORIGINAL THIREEEN
SATURDAY, APRIL 8, 1972

What was going on in the world when The Original Thirteen — the very first Balloon Fiesta pilots — took to the Albuquerque skies? The Vietnam War raged on, airline hijackings were almost commonplace, Apollo 16's date with the moon was already in count-down, and the Dow Jones Industrial 30 had just rallied to 962. The movie "Dirty Harry" starring Clint Eastwood, was in its third week. A brand new Pontiac Catalina sold for $3,644 and a Chevy Nova cost only $2,799; and one could purchase a hot air balloon for $4,995.

In New Mexico, it was the third year of low water supply due to mild weather and early mountain run-off. But there was no drought in New Mexico politics as House and Senate candidates filed for the 1972 election. In Los Alamos, April 8th was Clinton P. Anderson Day as Los Alamos National Labs named its new Meson Facility for the U.S. Senator.

In Albuquerque, KOB 770 AM Radio's 50th anniversary was destined to include the country's newest sport, a hot air balloon race. With urging from Dick McKee, KOB's general manager, Sidney

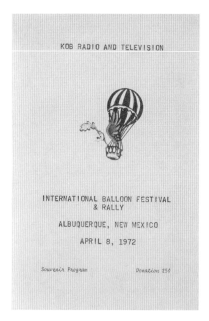

KOB RADIO AND TELEVISION

INTERNATIONAL BALLOON FESTIVAL
& RALLY

ALBUQUERQUE, NEW MEXICO

APRIL 8, 1972

Souvenir Program   *Donation 25¢*

The program for what is now considered to be the first Balloon Fiesta.

Cutter organized a southwestern-style, BFA-sanctioned Hare-and-Hound race (Roadrunner-Coyote race). Billed as "The First Annual KOB Radio & Television International Balloon Festival," it was to be the largest ballooning event in North America.

Sid Cutter is a life-long native of Albuquerque and an aviation veteran. He was a flight instructor before joining the Air Force in 1955 where he served five years as a jet pilot. On February 5, 1962, even though it would be nine more years before he saw his first balloon, Sid was issued an FAA balloon certificate. It read "Free Balloon Pilot—Hot Air Balloons Only." In 1971, while still operating Cutter Flying Service, he purchased one of Albuquerque's first hot air balloons, founded the Albuquerque Aerostat Ascension Association (AAAA or Quad A) and became a distributor for a major balloon manufacturer. He flew the *Roadrunner* balloon in the "First Albuquerque Balloon Fiesta." After staging the first two World Hot Air Balloon Championships, he was awarded the Fédération Aéronautique Internationale's (FAI) Montgolfier Diplome for the year 1975 for service to ballooning. In 1978 and 1986, he won the U.S. National Hot Air Balloon Championships. AAAA

has honored Albuquerque's "Father of Ballooning" with the Sid Cutter Traveling Trophy.

For the "First Fiesta," Sid called the Balloon Federation of America's Competition Director, Bob Waligunda, who facilitated the invitations for Albuquerque's inaugural ballooning event. Sid had only ten days to organize the balloon race, and somehow managed to schedule 21 balloons. Unfortunately, air freight problems in Los Angeles and a snowstorm in Chicago reduced the count to 13. Sid recalls "There were only about 40 balloons in the world at that time."

KOB's Tom Rutherford had been assigned to assist with the balloon portion of the radio station's 50th anniversary promotion. At the launch site were several celebrities, including Penny Marshall, who had attended UNM with Linda Rutherford. Penny's then-husband Rob Reiner was also on hand as a favor to Tom who launched his first campaign for the New Mexico State Senate, and indeed he did become the youngest person ever elected to the Senate. Rob was starring as "Meathead" in the new TV hit comedy *All in the Family*. Penny had not starred in *Laverne and Shirley* yet, but had a recurring role in some episodes of *The Odd Couple*. The late Slim Pickens, the Western movie star, happened to be in town for a land sales promotion on behalf of Tom's neighbor, Ruben Rodríquez, who had offered to host a barbeque for the pilots. The *Albuquerque Tribune* carried a photo of Slim that evening, waving to the throng at Coronado Center. Shortly after the Roadrunner-Coyote Balloon Race, KOB assigned Tom to assist Sid in bringing the First World Hot Air Balloon Championships to Albuquerque.

After 24 years as a New Mexico State Senator,

Tom retired as the Senate majority floor leader. He stayed with World Balloons until 1978 when he made an unsuccessful bid for the Lieutenant Governor's office. He was elected to the Bernalillo County Commission where he served two 4-year terms. After graduating from law school, Tom focused on administrative law and governmental affairs. Tom stays involved in the Fiesta as one of the voices behind the launch field microphone.

On April 7th, the *Albuquerque Journal* promoted the race, estimating 16 balloons would launch from the vacant lot west of Coronado Center. In the end, 13 balloons actually inflated, the first being the *Roadrunner*, Quad A's club balloon, with Sid as pilot and AAAA president Don Draper as co-pilot. Then at 7:30 am, Governor Bruce King fired the starting gun and 12 competing Coyote balloons launched before 20,000 spectators. The crowd surged against the rope perimeter which eventually gave way on the east side. The balloons drifted north, trailing advertising banners, and many spectators followed by car to the landing sites near the Albuquerque Academy.

Don Kersten – Fort Dodge, IA. The late Don Kersten was a lawyer and an Air Force veteran (1948-1952). He had been a licensed pilot since July 1965 and in this event flew a white Piccard balloon with two blue bands at the equator. Named *Merope* after his wife, this Coyote balloon was about fourth in the pack to launch.

One of Don's epic balloon flights occurred at the Indianapolis Speedway in 1968. There, his high wind collision with an occupied outhouse resulted in the first lawsuit against a balloonist; the occupant sued for loss of honor. Don went on to

Don Kersten in Merope *waves to Albuquerque's first balloon crowd.*

serve as the BFA President (1969-1971 and 1975-1977).

As immediate Past President of BFA and a FAI delegate in 1972, Don was asked to search for a site for the First World Hot Air Balloon Championships. Don urged Sid and Tom Rutherford to form an organization to bid Albuquerque as the host site. They created World Balloon Championships, Inc. "It wasn't until later that we learned no one else had bid, or even been invited to bid for this event," Tom recalls. Nevertheless, Albuquerque was secured as the host city for the 1973 event. Don Kersten died in 1998 at age 73.

Oscar Kratz – Tucson, AZ. Piloting another of the Coyote balloons was the late Oscar Kratz. It can be said that he is indirectly responsible for one of Albuquerque's first resident hot air balloon. In 1971, Sid wanted to rent a balloon for his mother's birthday at Cutter Flying Service. Oscar owned the first certified Raven AX-8 but it was too big for the hangar and his rental fee was $500. Instead, Sid bought a new Raven that he planned to use to advertise the party by tying it up outside. Sid says, "Oooo, how we learn!" Thanks to Oscar's "high" rent, N1951R became one of the first modern hot air balloons to call Albuquerque home.

Bill Cutter – Phoenix, AZ. Flying another Coyote balloon was Sid's older brother Bill. Upon request, the FAA issued Bill his balloon pilot license in 1963. He is a native of Albuquerque, an Army veteran (1955-1957) and co-owner of Cutter Avia-

Bill Cutter prepares to chase his younger brother Sid.

tion. This southwest aviation company, which now operates in eight locations, was established by Bill's father in 1928. His son now operates the company.

At the First Fiesta, Bill flew N1951R, the patriotic red, white and blue Raven balloon with gold bunting and white stars against a blue top. This is the balloon that he and Sid used at their mother's 1971 birthday celebration. He was the third Coyote to take to the air and like most trailed a long banner. Bill has not flown balloons for about five years and does not recall many details of that First Fiesta. "At my age—I'm 75—I'm not supposed to have a memory." Bill distinguished himself in balloon competition in the early 70s, placing third in the 1972 Nationals, fourth in the 1973 Nationals and second in the 1973 World Hot Air Balloon Championships in Albuquerque. Bill is still flying charters out of Phoenix for Cutter Aviation.

Dennis Floden – Flint, MI. A stockbroker and financial consultant, Denny Floden became a licensed balloonist in February 1969. At age 32, he won the U.S. National Balloon Championships in Indianola, Iowa, in 1971 and piloted a red, white and blue Raven balloon decorated with patriotic eagles and pennants in the First Fiesta as the reigning U.S. Champion. In his early years, he flew under the pseudonym "Capt. Phogg." Coincidentally, 1972, the year of Albuquerque's First Fiesta, was also the 100th anniversary of Jules Verne's fantasy novel *Around the World in Eighty Days* with Capt. Phileas Fogg.

Denny once said, "Ballooning gives you a sense of freedom, an ability to escape your cares and woes into another world." In 1973, Denny joined Bill

Cutter, Tom Oerman and Bruce Comstock on the U.S. team at the First World Hot Air Balloon Championships in Albuquerque. He won the title and the distinction of becoming the world's first champion balloonist. Denny used to say it takes "a little bit of skill and a lot of luck" to excel in balloon competition.

Denny was a balloon sales distributor and successful commercial balloonist. He designed Kellogg's first *Tony the Tiger* balloon and for 22 years led his *Gr-r-reat Tony* Balloon Team in the operation of one of the first special-shape commercial balloons. Now in his late 60s, Denny Floden is retired from the financial world and the world of commercial and competitive ballooning. He says he was a "card-carrying Michigan snowbird" for some time but now spends most of his time as a boater and real estate investor in Bradenton Beach, FL.

Bill Murtorff – Corpus Christi, TX. The late Bill Murtorff was an aeronaut extraordinaire. He was an Army veteran, having served from 1955 to 1958. While operating a water sports store in Corpus Christi, he became infatuated with hot air ballooning. As a student of Derek Howard, Bill received his balloon pilot license in July 1971. Derek remembers "Wild Bill," as he was affectionately known, as being so enthusiastic about ballooning that he would be around a long time. Indeed, Bill and his wife Mary were regular participants in the first 25 Albuquerque Balloon Fiestas.

On that special day in Albuquerque in 1972, Bill was fresh from a victory in the Florida Balloon Championships. His balloon, *Smile*, N22US, was the second Coyote balloon to launch. Bill received

AAAA's Sid Cutter Traveling Trophy in 1977 and he was BFA President during the period 1979-1981. He retired in Mexico where he died in 1998 at age 64 but his name lives in a place of honor in the BFA as the Bill Murtorff Aviation Education Scholarship.

Carter Twedt's Mike-Mike *inflates*

Donald Piccard – Newport Beach, CA. Don is the son of pioneer aeronauts Jean and Jeannette Piccard. He had been flying balloons since the 40s and is a pioneer in his own right. In the Navy, he served at Lakehurst, NJ in WWII and later in the Korean War. In 1947, he received the nation's first Free Balloon Pilot Certificate. He made numerous epic balloon flights and was awarded the Montgolfier Diplome for the year 1962 for his record altitude flight in a "poly-cluster" balloon. Don is credited with many of the innovations we see today in the modern hot air sport balloon.

He started a balloon manufacturing company in Newport Beach, California in 1964, so at the time of Albuquerque's First Fiesta, he claimed Newport Beach as home. Having flown in mile-high Albuquerque before, Don says, "I had flown over 30,000 ft. but launching there when you are accustomed to sea level needs to be taken into account." He remembers that "most of Albuquerque was empty lots then." Indeed, there was little development north of Montgomery and east of Juan Tabo where most of the Coyote balloons landed.

41

Matt Wiederkehr and Don Kersten rise in search of the Roadrunner balloon.

Don was one of the last to launch but he flew *The Spirit of 76*, N76US, to a first place finish, landing only 184 feet from the deflated *Roadrunner* balloon that Sid had left spread out as a giant target. Don had a ripout landing with a long drag across the mesa as Albuquerqueans rushed to grab his basket and as a helicopter hovered a few hundred yards away. That winning balloon was made for Burns, Burke and Morton of Gardena, CA and George Morton was getting his first ride. "It had two gi-

ant burners and two rip panels," recalls Don. "It was ideal for that flight. Dr. George, the met guy, was perfect and I paid attention to him."

Don was referring to Dr. George Fischbeck, the popular Albuquerque weatherman on KOB-TV from the early 60s until our First Fiesta when he was recruited by KABC-TV in Hollywood. He once said, "Take every opportunity you can get and value every friend you can get too, because between the two, you're headed to success."

Dr. George, as he was fondly known, graduated from the University of New Mexico in 1955 and worked a few years as a school teacher. He launched his television career at KNME-TV in Albuquerque by hosting a children's science program. He rarely missed an opportunity to educate his viewers on the subject of weather. His enthusiasm and encyclopedic knowledge of meteorology and the earth sciences were astounding. Dr. George's weather forecasts were intermingled with corny quips and silly bits of humor but were never scripted.

In 1977, he won the UNM Alumni Association Award of Distinction. Dr. George loved hot air balloons. In the mid-80s, the legendary meteorologist served as the honorary balloonmeister for the Rancho California Balloon & Wine Festival. In 1996, the weather veteran finally retired and in 2003 he was awarded an Emmy, the prestigious Academy of Television Arts & Sciences' Governors Award for lifetime achievement. He occasionally returns home to Albuquerque to attend the Balloon Fiesta. Now at 85, Dr. George volunteers as a docent at the Los Angeles Zoo.

Gene Dennis – Grand Blanc, MI. When Gene got into ballooning, he owned his own electrical contracting business that was geared to support the automotive industry in Michigan. His balloon instructor was Denny Floden, who also instructed Bruce Comstock, just before Denny won the 1971 Nationals. Gene and Denny had only one balloon between them. Both made it through the qualifying rounds but a toss of the coin put Denny in the basket instead of Gene.

After flying balloons with Denny Floden, Gene adopted the name "Captain Phair Weather." He claimed that the excellent flying conditions at the 1972 Fiesta were not the work of George Fischbeck, with his high altitude millibar charts, but it was he who ordered the day's good weather.

Gene recalls lifting off with Tom Oerman as his passenger. Tom's balloon never made it to Albuquerque because of the Chicago snowstorm. Gene's flight connections through Chicago were also cancelled but he drove to Detroit and caught a direct flight to Albuquerque. As for the 1972 race, Gene says "My balloon was a Raven® with red and white stripes, blue equator and yellow top. We landed somewhere in the boonies. The next day, several of us flew from the west mesa and drifted over the Rio Grande."

Gene placed 6th in the qualifying rounds for the 1973 World Championships, being edged out by Denny Floden, Tom Oerman and Bill Cutter. He returned to Albuquerque again for the 1974 Balloon Fiesta and again last year. He and his wife Janice visited the Balloon Museum and the old launch site at Coronado where Macy's is today. He has not been active for 10 years but his two sons are avid balloonists. Gene and Janice still reside in Grand Blanc, MI.

Matt Wiederkehr – St. Paul, MN. Matt was an engineer when he got into ballooning. He and his wife Bobbie operated a balloon sales distributorship and staged the hot air balloon competition at the annual St. Paul Winter Carnival. Matt and his daughters, Denise and Donna, set over 40 world ballooning records.

The first Coyote balloon to launch was Matt's blue and white balloon, N1926R, with co-pilot Denise and a long banner trailing below the basket. They made a classic ripout landing among cholla cactus on the east mesa, stopping dead in their tracks in a matter of seconds. As was customary in those days, all of the pilots in the First Fiesta wore helmets. Bobbie recalls, "At first everyone thought we won the race. Suddenly the winds changed and the Piccards won even though they were off course until the end." Matt and Denise ended up in third place.

Wilma Piccard – Newport Beach, CA. Don's wife, Willie, is an accomplished balloonist. She set the A-1 distance record for male and female using a single cell Mylar balloon. The male record has since been taken. As the only female pilot in the First Fiesta, Willie flew solo in *Gypsy*, N10TA, which later went to Bruce Comstock and helped him win the Nationals. Don recalls, "It was a super balloon, especially for the time, and gave Willie no trouble." She placed second, landing 206 feet from the *Roadrunner*. Don adds, "It was a kick for us to take first and second." Don and Willie now live in Minneapolis, MN.

Brent Stockwell – Daly City, CA. As a licensed commercial balloonist since 1970, Brent has participated in many hot air and gas balloon races around

Carter Twedt and Don Piccard climb into Albuquerque's crystal-blue sky.

the world. At the time of Albuquerque's inaugural ballooning event, he had been working on establishing the first FAA-approved balloon flight school in the U.S. Brent has been operating an FAA-certified balloon repair station since 1974. He has been active in the BFA for more than three decades and has received numerous BFA and FAA awards.

At the First Fiesta, his small AX-4 balloon, *Firebird*, N14US, was one of the last Coyotes to launch. It trailed a Rich Ford banner. Other sponsors of the First Fiesta included Cactus Realty, Galles Chevrolet, Horizon Corporation, Melloy Datsun, Pedal 'n Spoke, Vickers Petroleum and Watchworld.

Brent's balloon ran out of fuel before reaching the target *Roadrunner* balloon. He and his wife, Christine Kalakuka, authored several ballooning books while operating their flight school and repair station in Manteca, CA. Sadly, Christine passed away earlier this year. Brent still flies balloons and still operates their long-standing balloon business in Manteca.

Carter Twedt – Carson City, NV. Carter, an American Airlines pilot, with his crew chief, Pat Arthur, lifted off in a yellow Raven AX-6 with a red band at the equator sporting a string of white stars. A banner promoting Rich Ford dangled from the basket. This is the balloon that was used in Walt Disney's "High Flying Lowe" about Professor Thaddeus Lowe, the Civil War aeronaut who conducted aerial reconnaissance for the Union Army. N4MM or *Mike-Mike* as Carter calls the balloon (M-M for Mickey Mouse) was made up to look like a gas balloon in the Disney movie.

As for the 1972 race, "We brought our entire crew and the envelope in two Cessnas but we had to ship the gondola," says Carter. They placed 6th overall. Carter and Pat made a high-wind landing on the Sandia Pueblo Reservation and ended up hauling the balloon out piece by piece.

Carter retired from American Airlines in 1994 but he still flies—not jets, not balloons, but paragliders. His wife Peggy was also a licensed balloon pilot and made many commercial flights. Nevada Skydivers showed a special interest in *Mike-Mike*. Carter says, "The whole club wanted to jump so there have been at least 50 jumps from our old balloon." He and Peggy sold *Mike-Mike* several years ago but it reportedly is still around and is actually inflated on special occasions. Carter and Peggy still reside in Carson City.

Karl Stefan – Palestine, TX. Karl is a graduate of the Naval Academy and a WWII veteran, having retired in 1960 after 20 years in naval aviation. He made his first gas balloon flight in 1956 and his first hot air balloon flight in 1961. After teaching Chauncey Dunn how to fly balloons in Colorado

(Karl was working at the National Center for Atmospheric Research in Boulder at the time), they flipped a coin to see who would attempt a new altitude record. Karl won and reached 31,000 feet before his oxygen mask froze. Three days later, Chauncey, with a heater in his oxygen mask, set a new AX-8 record by reaching 33,000 feet.

Karl received the coveted Montgolfier Diplome for the year 1971 for service to ballooning. With Tracy Barnes and Dodds Meddock, this aeronautical engineer co-founded a highly successful balloon manufacturing company in Statesville, NC and later entered an airship manufacturing business that was not nearly as successful.

Now at age 91, Karl does not recall serving as the Safety Officer in 1972, but he distinctly remembers trailing a very long banner. Of his rapid ascent in his AX-6, *Star of Texas*, N1950R, to deploy the banner, he said, "I kept climbing and so turned the burner off, but I could still hear its roar. I then looked over the side of my basket and realized the roar was from the crowd below." Karl's flight ended with a ripout landing punctuated by two hard bounces.

He served as the U.S. delegate to the FAI Balloon Commission for well over a decade and had the pleasure of announcing Montgolfier awards to many other American balloonists (beginning with his first award announcement to this author). He also served as FAI Balloon Commission President from 1984 to 1994. Sid Cutter succeeded Karl as the U.S. delegate. Today, Karl and his wife Lucy live in Fort Collins, CO.

There was a reunion of The Original Thirteen on September 28, 1996 at Coronado Center. Wil-

Most of the "original 13" pilots who flew in the 1972 "International Balloon Festival at a 20th anniversary media event in Albuquerque in 1991.

lie Piccard was unable to attend and Oscar Kratz was represented by his widow Patty at this special Silver Anniversary celebration.

It was the late Tom Dunn, KOB Radio producer, director and morning show host, who said "When disc jockeys put on a show you can expect a windbag promotion." And what a promotion it was—not just for KOB but for ballooning in Albuquerque. The story of this inaugural ballooning event was carried by that evening's Albuquerque Tribune as front page news, and that was just the beginning as work commenced on the World Balloon Championships. As the forerunner of the annual Albuquerque International Balloon Fiesta, that first "windbag promotion" has become known as the "First Albuquerque Balloon Fiesta" and those balloon pilot pioneers have landed themselves in ballooning history books as "The Original Thirteen."

❏ Dick Brown, 2007

Some of the "First Ladies" of ballooning, taken at Ponderosa Studios, Virginia City, Nevada, during the 1977 National Balloon Rally. Top row L to R: Janice Hebrlee, Sandy MacDonald, Lori McLain, Connie March, Charlotte Kinney; middle row: Ruth McLain, Sally Vale; bottom row: Sandy Brannam, Nikki Caplan, and Marge Ruppenthal.

The First Ladies
of New Mexico Ballooning

Ed Yost, who lives near Vadito, New Mexico, is internationally recognized as the father of the modern hot-air balloon. Sid Cutter, from Albuquerque, is unquestionably the father of the largest ballooning event in the world, the Albuquerque International Balloon Fiesta (AIBF). Don Draper was the first President of what is now the largest ballooning club in the world, the Albuquerque Aerostat Ascension Association (AAAA). Impressive men with relentless enthusiasm for ballooning. But who was the mother? Who were the female pioneers?

At least in terms of holding a license, we think that Virginia Cutter was the first female balloon pilot in New Mexico. Virginia, along with her sons Bill and Sid, was an experienced fixed-wing pilot. In the summer of 1962, the three completed a Federal Aviation Administration (FAA) form requesting a balloon rating on their pilots' certificates, and received them without balloon training or examination (Sid confesses that they had never seen a balloon). This was perfectly legal in 1962. The FAA did not begin to set down separate specific requirements for balloon ratings until the late 1960's.

The next chapter relates to three friends, one of whose husband decided to buy a hot-air balloon for his wife for her birthday, as well as for a promotional gimmick for his automobile dealership. The balloon was a yellow Raven AX-6 with giant smiling blackbirds on three sides, each with the Chevrolet logo on its belly. Ed Black was the car dealer, and the balloon's name was *Smiley*. This was in late 1972, after the first gathering of modern hot-air balloons in New Mexico at Coronado Center in April of 1972.

Loretto Black was Ed's wife, and along with her

49

Ed Black's balloon Smiley

two friends Joan Florance and Bev Grady (all three were fixed-wing pilots), became the first trained women hot-air balloon pilots in New Mexico. Their instructor was Gary Higman, who was an employee of Sid Cutter at Cutter Aviation. Their training occurred mostly in *Smiley*, and according to Joan and Bev and Buddy Rice (Buddy was employed by Ed Black, was also a fixed-wing pilot, and was nominally in charge of the Ed Black Chevrolet balloon after family and friends got their balloon ratings), two of the three received their balloon ratings on the same day, March 16, 1973, from Jim Valentine, head of the Albuquerque FAA Flight Standards District Office. This was Jim's first check ride actually in a balloon. Due to some broken ribs weeks earlier, Loretto did not fly with Joan and Bev that day. Loretto received her balloon rating 5-5-73, also from Jim Valentine. Joan still lives in Albuquerque, and Bev and husband Gil live in Silver City.

The next several women balloon pilots became interested in ballooning, as did their male counterparts, due to the annual ballooning events in Albuquerque. Jonelle Shepherd had her first balloon ride in *Mellow Yellow*, an experimental Stokes hot-air balloon, in late 1972. This balloon was purchased by Don Marshall, John and Carol Davis, Bobby John, Jerry Whitlow and Jim and Jonelle Shepherd. Husband Jim, John Davis and Roger Hoppe were her instructors. Jonelle remembers that she got her license the same day as Pat Barz, 10-28-74, from Sid Cutter. It was foggy that day, and she had forgotten her instruments, so Sid suggested they land and get his instruments. As they descended quickly through the fog, Sid spotted some powerlines and yelled, "Burn, burn!" They never got Sid's instruments. Jonelle says it's the only time she ever saw Sid excited.

Paula O'Brien Dougherty had her first balloon ride 2-17-73, with Bob Sparks (he was "Captain America") in a McArthur balloon, and again the next day in an early Semco. She was issued her student balloon license 5-31-74 and her balloon rating 7-8-74, having been trained by Sylvain Segal in his Piccard balloon *Scarlet O'Aira*. [Paula and several others, including Syl Segal, Jon Ashworth and Bill Hyde, bought Pat Chowning's red, white and blue Piccard balloon, N35US. Paula's first husband David had crewed with "Chowning's Chargers."] Paula dated Tracy Barnes occasionally, and bought one of his balloons with Elaine Kramer (named *Ladies Choice*) in which Paula piloted its maiden flight 1-23-77.

Jane Martindale was in the same AAAA early-1973 "class" with J.W. Byrd, Tom McConnell and Allan Tonkin (Sid Cutter's brother-in-law). Her instructors were Greg and Mark Wilson, Don

Draper and Paul Enz, and she got her license in late 1973 with Sid Cutter as examiner, flying the first AAAA club balloon, N1954R, *Roadrunner One*. She remembers the July 4th, 1973 AAAA scavenger hunt when Rusty Rutherford, Tom Rutherford's little brother, was on her scavenger team.

Carol Rymer Davis had her first ride the end of June 1973, soloed 9-23-73 and earned her balloon rating 11-24-73. Pat Barz had her first balloon ride in the early spring of 1973, first training flight 9-16-73, soloed 10-20-74 and took her check ride with Sid Cutter 10-28-74. Her instructors were husband Don (they now live in Arvada, Colorado), Tom McConnell, Tom Donnelly, Bob Ruppenthal, Sid Cutter and Wally Book.

Pat Barz, Marge Ruppenthal and Linda Rutherford all took their training at about the same time. Pat remembers the three of them studying together for the written test, and all three receiving higher marks on that exam than their husbands (or so goes the story). Marge had her first balloon ride with Tom Donnelly and Dick Wirth, received instruction from husband Bob and from Don Barz, was balloon-rated in May 1975, and flew the early Thunder balloons sold by Bob. Linda flew Raven *Jeremy*, named after Tom and Linda's son, and Pat flew their Raven *Black Magic*. Pat and Don Barz were partners in the first *Zia*, [June, 1973] with Tom and Mary McConnell. Bob and Marge now live in Chama, while Carol and John Davis live in Denver.

Judy Baron took her first ride with Wally Book sometime in 1973, and received her hot-air balloon rating in 10-20-74 from FAA examiner Sid Cutter. Her instructors were Wally Book and Joe Jackson. Judi Rice, Trudy Farr, Emily Wenz from

Los Alamos and Suzy Schmidt took their balloon training in 1974 or 1975.

Neida Courtney Naumberg had her first balloon ride in August 1973, after she and then-husband Norm Courtney

Virginia Cutter in 1973.

and nine other couples ordered a Semco (*Tumbleweed*) from Mark Semich in early 1973. Neida soloed 3-13-77 and got her rating 10-4-77. Her instructor was Norm Courtney. Neida remembers a particularly laid-back student pilot by the name of Flip Wilson who had a windy landing in a tree in April, 1981.

Donna Brown was very involved in ballooning, crewing for her husband Dick, helping with the writing and editing of the *Cloudbouncer* and serving as an official at various races. She took lessons, and even soloed on 8-23-75, but chose not to get her balloon license. (However, some contend the flight wasn't really a "solo" because she had a scorpion in the basket with her.)

The third Fiesta, in February 1974, saw Buddy Rice and Joan Florance flying the *Smiley* balloon, not from the Fairgrounds, but from a parking lot just outside the Fairgrounds, off the northeast corner. Sid had decided to declare all balloons who had commercial logos on them "commercial," and decided to charge them $1000 entry fee, unlike the private balloons entered. Mr. Black and Mr. Rice were not happy with that arrangement, and decided to boycott the Fiesta, but since a movie was being made about the *Smiley* balloon, they decided to launch not inside the Fairgrounds, but close. The opening Saturday saw the *Smiley* balloon rise across Louisiana Boulevard and chase the hare (*Roadrunner*) balloon. Sure enough, they landed right next to the hare, and won first prize, even though they were not officially entered! Joan claims that she was the pilot-in-command. So does Buddy.

Suzi Flynt had her first balloon ride in February, 1974, when she flew with Dick Waggoner and Rolla Hinkle in Roswell in the *NMMI* balloon, received instruction from her husband Bill and from Bill Glen, and got her rating in September, 1976.

Sue Corlew had her first balloon ride in May, 1974, with Jim Shepherd in his Semco *Captain America* in Midland, Texas. She and her husband Mike bought their yellow and brown Raven Rally *Dust Devil* in May 1974, and had her first official lesson in Farm-

Joan Florance (left) and Bev Grady (right), with Buddy Rice on the far right.

ington on Memorial Day, 1974. She received her balloon rating in early 1975 from an El Paso, Texas FAA examiner who refused to ride in the balloon with her. She remembers many exciting flights, such as flying 220 miles from Lubbock to Amarillo in 2½ hours. She said she never had a "stand-up" landing until she and Mike moved to Albuquerque.

Sheri Bachtell (now Sheri Moore) had her first balloon ride with John Davis in *Raggedy Ann* in October, 1975. Hal Schlather (third President of AAAA) instructed her in her and her husband's balloon *Desert Groundhog* in spring, 1976. She soloed 4-24-76 and received her balloon rating from Bob Ruppenthal 5-21-76. Sheri instructed her now husband Jerrie after 1983.

Elaine Kramer Roderick had her first flight in October 1975, with "some guy from Houston named Larry." She crewed for Mark Wilson during 1976, met Paula O'Brien and the two of them purchased *Ladies Choice* in January 1977. Elaine first flew in *Ladies Choice* 1-29-77. She received her private balloon rating 6-11-77 and her commercial 10-6-81.

Both Molly Grady and sister Beth Grady Dixon Baurick took lessons and soloed, but never bothered to get their license. This was in 1975. Molly's friend Sandy McDonald received her balloon rating in 1978. Her cousin Darryl Gunter was her instructor, and she had her FAA check ride from Clair Bennett.

Charlotte Kinney and Kathy Hart both had their first balloon rides with Darryl Gunter. Charlotte and John Lynch bought the brown and white Raven rally *Daytripper* in January 1977, and she received her balloon rating in early spring that year. She remembers the "BBB, a little club for female

balloonists" (one can only imagine what BBB stands for).

Sue Ellen Shaffer Osika crewed for the Shepherds in *Captain America* beginning in 1974, had her first official balloon instruction in August 1977 and got her private balloon rating in 1978. Her instructor was Charlotte Kinney.

Other early lady balloonists not already mentioned include Sally Chapel, Gay Jensen-James, now living in California, the late Phyllis McGuire from Angel Fire and Glenda Watson, now residing in Hawaii. There may be others who may contact the author after they find themselves not mentioned, and who will certainly give him a couple hits with the wet noodle.

Lady balloonists had many other accomplishments besides piloting balloons. For example, Betty Perkins, Sheri Bachtell Moore, Marge Ruppenthal, and Gail Short were early Presidents of AIBF, Linda Rutherford and Marge Ruppenthal were early AIBF Executive Directors, and Carol Davis, Connie March and Sue Hazlett held ballooning records in the mid to late-1970s. Neida Courtney and Charlotte Kinney were the first AIBF balloonmeistern (female balloonmeisters).

These New Mexico women were pioneers, and very much a part of the 1970's explosion of ballooning in the state that claims the largest and best balloon club in the world (AAAA) and the largest and best balloon event in the world (AIBF). Many were wives or friends of balloonists, but many others were just caught up in the fun and sport of hot-air ballooning. But regardless of motivation, all can be proud to be the First Ladies of New Mexico ballooning.

❏ Thomas McConnell, 2003

MASS ASCENSION

    From the beginning, the Balloon Fiesta's signature event has been the mass ascension. Under the careful control of the launch directors ("Zebras"), hundreds of balloons inflate and head skyward in rapid sequence, filling the launch field and the skies with colorful floating bubbles, the pulsating roar and heat of the burners, and the delighted cheers of spectators.

    A picture may be worth a thousand words—but actually being there, under a canopy of color created by the inflated balloons towering above and thrilling to the excitement as each soars aloft, is worth a million!

The World Comes to Albuquerque

Today, the Albuquerque International Balloon Fiesta is known worldwide as an event that emphasizes fun, flying and camaraderie over serious competition. It's ironic that the Fiesta got its start, in large measure, as an arena for that most serious of competitions, the World Championships.

Albuquerque got the nod as the host city for the world championships when Don Kersten, at the time the President of the Balloon Federation of America (BFA), asked the organizers of the 1972 "first Fiesta" if the city might be willing to bid for the World Championships. Sid Cutter and Tom Rutherford came up with a proposal, which they duly submitted to Kersten. Today, Cutter notes with a chuckle that Kersten didn't tell him that Albuquerque was the only city he'd approached!

Now that Albuquerque had the event, it had to figure out what to do with it. Ed Yost, one of the inventors of the airborne heater and today considered to be the father of modern hot-air ballooning, agreed to be the Clerk of the Course, or chief official (roughly the equivalent of today's Balloonmeister). He and Cutter went to work devising the "tasks"

the competitors would have to perform. Cutter remembers that many of their early ideas didn't pass muster with the authority governing international ballooning, the Fédération Aéronautique Internationale (FAI), because they involved maneuvers that the FAI considered to be too dangerous. ("And they were," admits Cutter.)

Eventually, they settled principally on a series of tasks that relied heavily on the use of an instrument known as a barograph. The barograph provides a continuous trace on a graph, showing the balloon's altitude at any given time in the flight. The pilot was required to fly a profile of ascents and descents to certain altitudes that followed an optimum pattern. Three of the four events were tied to the barograph.

The fourth, and today the best known, was the "Coyote-Roadrunner Race" (also sometimes known as the

"Roadrunner-Coyote Race"). A balloon, the "Roadrunner," launched first, flew for a while, then landed and set out a target. The "Coyote" balloons (the competitors) had to launch about 10 minutes after the Roadrunner and give chase in an effort to land as close to the Roadrunner's landing site as possible.

Another question was when and where the event should be held. The 1972 Fiesta had been held in April, which turned out to be a lousy month because of strong spring winds. The organizers looked at weather data and decided the second week of February would be a great time to hold the event (but stay tuned). The search for a site big enough and equipped to accommodate more than 130 balloons and thousands of spectators led to one logical site: the racetrack at the State Fairgrounds.

A myriad of other details had to be hammered out…logistics for ceremonies and parades…lodging, transportation, and chase crews for the pilots …schedules for both the World Championship events and for fun-flying "Fiesta" events for balloonists who were not World competitors. The weekends, as they are today, were reserved for ceremonial events and mass ascensions. The four World Championship tasks were scheduled for 8 a.m. on the weekdays. The Fiesta events for non-competing

Sid Cutter's Wile E Coyote® *Balloon, festooned with the famous cartoon characters, soars aloft as the "Roadrunner" (Hare) target balloon. The competitors – the "Coyotes" – took off in pursuit about 10 minutes later. Closest Coyote balloon to the Roadrunner's target wins!*

balloonists were set to go off at the incredibly late (for balloonists) hour of 11 a.m. Back in those days, balloonists were still learning that the longer you fly after sunrise, the more likely you are to run into trouble with atmospheric instability.

The FAI had ruled that each competing nation could send up to four competitors to the World Championships. Fourteen nations sent competitors: Sweden, the Netherlands, Belgium, France, Germany, Denmark, Great Britain, Switzerland, Australia, Canada, Ireland, Norway, Italy and the U.S. The United States delegation consisted of the 1972 national champion, Bruce Comstock, and three pilots who were chosen in competitions flown in Albuquerque the week before the World Championships: Tom Oerman, Denny "Captain Phogg" Floden and Bill Cutter (who is Sid's brother).

Finally, the time arrived, and balloonists and spectators from all over the country and the world started pouring into Albuquerque. The local hospitality purveyors had no idea what was about to hit them. They were overwhelmed. The call went out to local residents asking for help. Thousands of Albuquerqueans responded. Hundreds joined chase crews. Others, like Bob and Marge Ruppenthal, found bands of grubby balloonists on their

doorsteps, helmets, logbooks, valises, burners, and baskets in tow. "We had a ball," Marge remembers of the ten days one of the British teams spent encamped in her home. By the time they left, the Ruppenthals had bought a balloon and, like many others who caught the ballooning bug that week, were on their way to becoming one of Albuquerque's most prominent ballooning families.

Opening day dawned clear and bright. Flags, bands, and dignitaries paraded down the racetrack in front of a huge opening day crowd. Dozens of balloons headed skywards. People were in awe. The First World Championships were off to a great start.

On Monday, the competition began—and so did the challenges. The barograph tasks created a lot of controversy and protest. The bright, sunny, Chamber of Commerce weather deteriorated into snow squalls into which balloons all but vanished. When the winds were blowing towards the south, the State Fairgrounds turned out to be too close for comfort to the airport, and to a few other even more sensitive installations. Local balloonists still swap stories about perfectly innocent international pilots, toting cameras and unable to speak a word of English, facing gun-toting security guards after landing inside the quadruple fencing surrounding the super-secret Manzano Base.

But by the final mass ascension, the First World Championships were a spectacular success. Spectators loved it and, so, by and large, did the balloonists. The winner and first World Champion in hot-air ballooning was "Captain Phogg," Denny Floden of Flint, Michigan. Floden admitted that the most important factor in his victory was that he had spent time learning how to "fly the barograph" and honed his skills for this peculiar series of tasks.

The infield at the NM State Fairgrounds hosted the World Championships' distinguished international competitors. Spectators were not allowed on the launch field; they saw the show from the racetrack grandstand.

He admitted he did not do well in the one event that has survived the test of time and is still used extensively in competition, the Roadrunner-Coyote (or Hare and Hound) race. Floden has been a fixture at the Albuquerque Fiesta for most of its 30-year history and is best-known to recent Fiesta-goers as the pilot of *The G-r-r-eat Tony.*

With the success of the 1973 Worlds, Albuquerque was well on its way to carving a permanent niche in the ballooning world. The next year a group of citizens backed by Albuquerque Mayor Harry Kinney began the organization that would become today's Albuquerque International Balloon Fiesta, Inc. The 1974 Fiesta, featuring mostly local and domestic pilots and run on a relative shoestring, kept the tradition alive. The Fiesta had become an institution, and Albuquerque had become the "Hot Air Balloon Capital of the World."

❑ Kim Vesely, 2001

69

Ballooning, A "Spectator Sport"

Can You Steer a Balloon?

Winds determine a balloon's direction. Balloonists can steer a balloon, to a limited extent, by adjusting the balloon's altitude to catch different layers of wind, which may have different speeds and directions. If pilots want to move in a particular direction, they ascend or descend to these different layers and ride with the wind.

Flying in a balloon race may be easier than watching one.

At Indianapolis, you can sit still and the cars come round every couple of minutes or so.

At the Kentucky Derby, runners are considerate enough to come back and finish where they started.

Even an Olympic marathon runner knows where the finish line is going to be, 26 miles 385 yards later.

But balloons? Where they will wind up is anyone's guess. And for once a handicapper knows as much as the rider because the guy flying the balloon has no idea either.

Balloons will only go one way and that is the way the wind is blowing. Trouble is, the wind at ground level may be blowing exactly the opposite direction from the wind at 2,000 feet.

This is the one sport where the contestant sits still and the spectators do all the running.

Accessories for watching a balloon race should include a strong pair of shoes (and an extra pair of dry ones), binoculars, a co-driver in the car to keep an eye on the target, and a picnic lunch.

Veteran balloon race watchers also file away many mental tips. They know, for instance, that when the balloons take off after an hour or so's preparation from the field or shopping center parking lot, they are followed by a massive traffic jam as spectators rush to follow.

Another thing about balloon races is that many are scheduled for the early morning for favorable wind conditions. Starts at 7 a.m. are not unusual.

One of the good things about balloon races, however, is that everybody gets a great view without having to jostle for position.

In fact, ballooning as a spectator sport is definitely "looking up."

❏ Sid Cutter, 1973

Games Balloonists Play

Way back in 1972, when approached about bringing his lone balloon to KOB Radio's 50th anniversary celebration, Sid Cutter said, "Maybe we could get two or three other balloons. Maybe we could even have a balloon race." "So, what's a balloon race." "Well, I don't know . . . but I hear they have them . . . so I guess we can find out . . ."

Over the years, pilots and guests at Balloon Fiesta have had a lot of fun "finding out" about balloon competition. The very first Balloon Fiesta introduced the "hare and hound" competition—in true Albuquerque fashion dubbed the "Roadrunner-Coyote" race—where a target "Roadrunner" balloon would launch first and try to elude the "Coyote" balloons launching about ten minutes later. The balloon coming closest to the Roadrunner balloon won.

Other early Balloon Fiesta events included the "Le Mans," where balloonists raced to be first across an imaginary line, and competitions which re-quired pilots to fly a detailed altitude profile traced on an instrument called a barograph. An early favorite was the "tumbleweed drop," where balloonists were required to harvest a tumbleweed, launch a specified distance from a target, and drop the tumbleweed as close as possible to the center of the "X". Some of the tumbleweeds harvested for competition were the size of small houses and capable of doing as much damage if dropped in the wrong place as Dorothy's house did to the Wicked Witch of the East. The use of tumbleweeds as markers was soon "dropped" in favor of lighter items such as ping pong balls and film boxes. Today's markers

The "pole grab" is occasionally called the "key grab," because the prize atop the pole may be the keys to a new truck or car. Begun in 1978, for more than 30 years the pole grab has been a signature event featuring some of the Balloon Fiesta's most exciting moments. Pilots must launch at least one mile away from the field in any direction and use the winds to maneuver their balloon to the poles erected at Balloon Fiesta Park. Envelopes on top of the poles contain cash and prizes, and the pilot or passenger must cleanly grab the envelope while keeping their feet flatly on the floor of the basket.

(referred to as "baggies") are small bags of sand or seeds, with long streamers attached which can be dropped on or thrown to the "X."

Today's competitions require precision flying to targets on and off Balloon Fiesta Park. The colorful sight of balloons jockeying for position in the Pole Grab competition is one of the great spectacles of Balloon Fiesta and one of the most exciting events for guests. Balloonists earn points in daily contests, and the overall Balloon Fiesta champion is the pilot earning the most points throughout the week. While big prizes can be at stake—the 2009 champion Frank Dickey (see photo on p. 172) took home $10,000—the bragging rights are also nothing to sneeze at!

Competition flights take place on weekdays during the Balloon Fiesta, with pilots flying a series of "tasks." Competition is governed by a strict set of rules designed to promote a safe and fair contest. While flying into Balloon Fiesta Park, pilots must observe altitude limits and cannot descend below those minimums until within the flagged target area. Balloons hitting the ground are disqualified from the task.

While competitions are fun for pilots and guests alike, they also serve a larger purpose. In order to compete successfully, balloonists must pilot a craft as tall as a seven-story building and nearly as wide to an object as small as an envelope or a stake in the center of an "X." This requires finely honed navigation and flying skills and the concentration needed to reach a target while still remaining in control of the balloon. For nearly forty years the games balloonists play have promoted skill, safety, and fun for all.

❏ Kim Vesely, 2010

The "Balloon Fiesta Drop" (abbreviated, tongue-in-cheek, "BFD") requires pilots to launch a minimum of one mile away and drop markers on an "X"-shaped target on the field (photo above). Closest to the center of the "X" wins—and the difference is often measured in hundredths of an inch!

The "Double Drop" (photo on opposite page) is a variation of the Balloon Fiesta Drop, but with the challenge of having to drop two markers in order to earn a score. Two "V" shaped targets are set up facing each other in this manner: > <. The pilot must drop one baggie inside each "V"; markers closest to the point of the "V's" win. A drop outside the "V" does not score.

Fore! That object flying at the pin (in the photo above) isn't a golf ball—it's a baggie! In "Balloon Fiesta Golf," the center of the target is a flag-marked golf hole, and closest to the pin wins. This contest pays tribute to the fact that for most of the year the southern end of Balloon Fiesta Park is a golf driving range.

Balloonists also play card games from the air. In the "Balloon Fiesta Hold 'Em" competition, the targets are large playing cards, and pilots must try to build the best possible hand by dropping markers on oversized playing cards. In some years, "Balloon Fiesta Blackjack," a variation of this competition, has been staged.

The Cloudbouncer Balloon Rally

Because the third Albuquerque International Balloon Fiesta held in February 1974 was a money-loser for Sid Cutter, although a success in every other way, in December of 1974 Sid, President of World Balloon Championships, Inc., and Tom Rutherford, Vice-President, announced that there would be no Balloon Fiesta in February 1975.

By January, 1975, commitments to hold the event in Albuquerque were gaining ground, but if the Second World Balloon Championships were to be held, they would have to be in October, giving more time for financing and having a better weather record than February. So, to hold interest in Albuquerque ballooning, the Albuquerque Aeronaut Ascension Association (AAAA, the local balloon club created by Cutter), the Chamber of Commerce and various other volunteers agreed to host and stage a balloon rally in February at

Fairgrounds launch looking south, Saturday, February 22, 1975.

the State Fairgrounds. Diane Terry, Secretary of AAAA, sent out the balloonists' invitations January 30, and Harold Schlather, President of AAAA, and Harold Levin, chair of a special balloon promotion committee of the Albuquerque Chamber of Commerce, made the official press announcement February 12. The AAAA named the rally "Cloudbouncer" after the club's newsletter. Little did they know...

The morning of Saturday, February 22 dawned cold and cloudy, having snowed the day before, when 33

83

New Mexico, and eight out-of-state balloons registered for this event, assembled at the fairgrounds. At 7:30 a.m., a weather briefing predicted light and variable winds with possible snow showers. A hole in the clouds appeared, the sun shown briefly, and the race was on. Miss Albuquerque-Universe, Jonelle Bergquist, officially started the Roadrunner-Coyote Race by presenting John Davis, pilot of Sid Cutter's 105,000 cubic foot white *Coyote-Roadrunner* balloon, with a bottle of champagne. Weatherman Dick Edwards provided commentary on the event for the benefit of spectators.

It is apparent from personal recollections and newspaper clippings that some of the balloons on the official registration list did not fly, and some not on the list did fly. For example, Carol Rymer Davis did not fly *Queen Celeste* because on the way to the fairgrounds that morning the uprights accidentally fell out of the balloon truck on 1-40 and were smashed by a semi. Carol instead flew Terry Pierce's *A.M.F.* with Pat Barz and Connie Busse (one of the first all-female flights in a New Mexico official race) and Bill Busse flew as a passenger with Don Barz in *Black Magic* because he had broken both ankles some months earlier, and was still recovering. (This was not the dentist, Dr. Bill Bussey, from Longview, Texas.)

John Davis, pilot-in-command of the *Roadrunner*, with passengers Ray Tillery (later to become President of AAAA) and Larry Merry (long-time crew person, observer and event-volunteer), ascended at about 8 a.m. in the big white Raven S-105, N1951R, and immediately floated toward the southeast. One by one, the rest of the "Coyotes" ascended and attempted to follow the *Roadrunner*.

As soon as the balloons were in the air, snow squalls were spotted to the west, north and south, and clouds covered the mountains to the east. About half the "Coyote" balloons kept in a southeasterly direction, following the *Roadrunner*, while the other half, seeing the low-hanging clouds and snow squalls, headed low toward the east-northeast.

Davis, after flying for about an hour, was becalmed over the east end of Runway 26 at the International Airport, sometimes in the clouds, sometimes not, while his passengers were busy throwing bits of Kleenex over the side to determine wind direction below them. Cleverly having an aircraft radio on board, Davis called the tower to explain what was happening. Tower personnel told him to move away from the airport. Davis explained that the balloon would go in the direction and at the speed where God wanted it to go. Not happy with that response, the tower again insisted Davis remove himself from Runway 26. Davis replied that he was more than 1,000 feet above ground level and that perhaps airplanes could land beneath the balloon. The three intrepid balloonists in the "Roadrunner" balloon were entertained by sounds (when they were in the clouds) or sights (when they could see) of large aircraft landing beneath them.

Dick Brown in *Blue Dragon*, Bill Douglas in *La Desengrapadora* and several others chasing the *Roadrunner* were in similar straits. Brown landed on a taxiway at the airport. Douglas had as passengers Suzie Schmidt and his daughter, Dianna, who was 8 years old at the time. It was so cold by the time Davis had landed that Douglas had given his jacket to his daughter, periodically putting her feet in his armpits to keep her warm. *La Desendgrapa-*

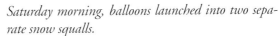

Saturday morning, balloons launched into two separate snow squalls.

out of the clouds and landed next to Davis, Tillery and Merry, and won the race.

Carol, Pat as co-pilot, and Connie, in *A.M.F.*, landed on Manzano Base, having also flown through the snow squalls chasing John. They were met by armed military, who confiscated Pat's camera. It has never been determined exactly what *A.M.F.* abbreviates.

dora went from almost motionless to fast in a couple seconds, having been caught in a strong eddy from the falling snow and unstable air, landing rather unceremoniously (after almost hitting a house and flying between trees) in a field south of the Sandia Base Officers' Club near Eubank Boulevard.

Davis in the *Roadrunner* balloon finally moved far enough away from the runway to land in a schoolyard on Sandia Base. Dave Sibila, from Denver, flying the original *Grape Escape*, N51518, came

Wally Book, flying *Chariot of the Gods*, a Raven S-50, also went south, and was in a snow squall so heavy that the only way he could tell where he was flying was to holler to one of his chase crew right below him. Wally stayed high enough to clear trees and powerlines, was instructed by his team of people in trucks, who were communicating with each other, about the path ahead and he finally landed in a schoolyard on the base next to the mother of all jungle gyms. He says those Military Police were quite understanding.

Jon Ashworth, flying *Harvey Wallbanger*, was also intent on winning the Roadrunner-Coyote

Dick Brown's Blue Dragon *balloon over the state fairgrounds.*

race that day, even with ice on his gauges and snow in his face. As he approached Davis in the big white Roadrunner balloon, somewhere north of the airport, he heard the noise from a balloon burner over his left shoulder. Jim Baldo, in *Wind Bag*, as was his standard practice, whizzed down past Ashworth so fast that the Doppler shift Baldo made sounded like a train going past. Not wanting to compete

with that, Jon drifted easterly and finally landed safely at Los Altos Golf Course.

Since Kurt Gottlieb was flying *Cactus Jack*, co-owner Bob Ruppenthal borrowed a Raven S-50 from Sid Cutter, and with Terry Adams (a British Royal Navy aircraft carrier pilot and member of the 1973 British hot-air balloon team), flew off as one of the "Coyote" balloons, and soon found the air unstable, with snow squalls coming in from the northwest. He approached the golf course near Wyoming and Lomas in northeast Albuquerque, made a cool approach ("cool" as in significant negative buoyancy, not "cool" as in modern teenage jargon) over a fence toward the open golf course, stopped just above the fence between Art Janpol Volkswagen and the golf course, reversed direction, and wiped out five brand new Volkswagen cars. Since both people in the gondola were pilots, one was burning and one was pulling the vent. Bob admitted he was on the vent and Terry was on the burner. Bob won. They were not hurt except for their egos.

Meanwhile, several other balloons were also experiencing their first flight in the snowy clouds. Drifting toward the northeast, Tom McConnell and then-student pilot Bill Glen in Zia attempted a landing at a schoolyard but were foiled more than once by the aerial acrobatics of air molecules being pulled downward with the falling snow and doing circles and eddies about 100 feet above ground level. Sylvain Segal in *Scarlet O'Aira* was unfortunate enough to land in a backyard west of Eubank between Parsifal and Salem Streets in northeast Albuquerque, where the envelope draped over powerlines and burned. No one was hurt. Mark Wilson in *Roadrunner I*, Tom McConnell in *Zia* and Linda

Rutherford in *Jeremy*, among others, landed in a large vacant lot in a snowstorm with two inches of snow on the balloon tops, water pouring into the gondolas from the melting snow. J.W. Byrd in *Wandering Star*, with son Jimmy, landed in an arroyo not far distant. All balloons and balloonists eventually landed safely. Shaken, but unbowed.

That night, pilots attempted to dry out their balloons in various ways. Bob Russell, pilot of *Marisol*, and Douglas, had dry balloons (more particularly, dry Velcro crown closures so necessary for safe flight) on Sunday morning, dried in Russell's warehouse. The McConnells and Byrds were not as successful in drying their balloons in their living rooms with the furnace on high.

Sunday, February 23, when a mass ascension was planned, was very cold, but clear. Not many spectators made it to the fairgrounds that day. Balloons were on their own, but were cleared to take off at pilot's discretion. Many balloons did not fly at all, some inflated and tethered, in order to dry out the envelopes and Velcro, and others had beautiful flights in fairly calm winds. Bill Douglas and Ray Toler in *La Desengrapadora*, for instance, flew for three hours, changing passengers more than once, and finally coming to rest in the eastern-most part of the Isleta Pueblo lands. Carol Davis and Pat Barz flew *Lucky 7*. The *Grape Escape* also flew on Sunday. *Scarlet O'Aira*, sadly, never flew again.

The event was a success in spite of the snowstorm, and the balloonists who flew that Saturday in the clouds and snow will never forget the experience. In fact, many of the stories are better now than 26 years ago. Following the now-famous, sometimes harrowing "Albuquerque International Snow Balloon Rally," money was obtained by the

Piccard balloon Mercedes II *owned and flown by Chuck Ray.*

Chamber of Commerce and WBC, from donors and sponsors, and with the help and encouragement of then-Mayor Harry Kinney and many others, the Second World Balloon Championships/Fourth Albuquerque International Balloon Fiesta went off without a hitch in October of 1975 at a new site, Simms Field, in northeast Albuquerque.

The February 1975, AAAA Cloudbouncer Rally was the last ballooning event held at the State Fairgrounds. The "Snow Rally" later became known as the AAAA Valentines Rally, and now survives as the AAAA Friends and Lovers Balloon Rally, the 27th having been held in February, 2001.

Some remember 1975 as the year they held two Balloon Fiestas.

❑ Tom McConnell, 1975

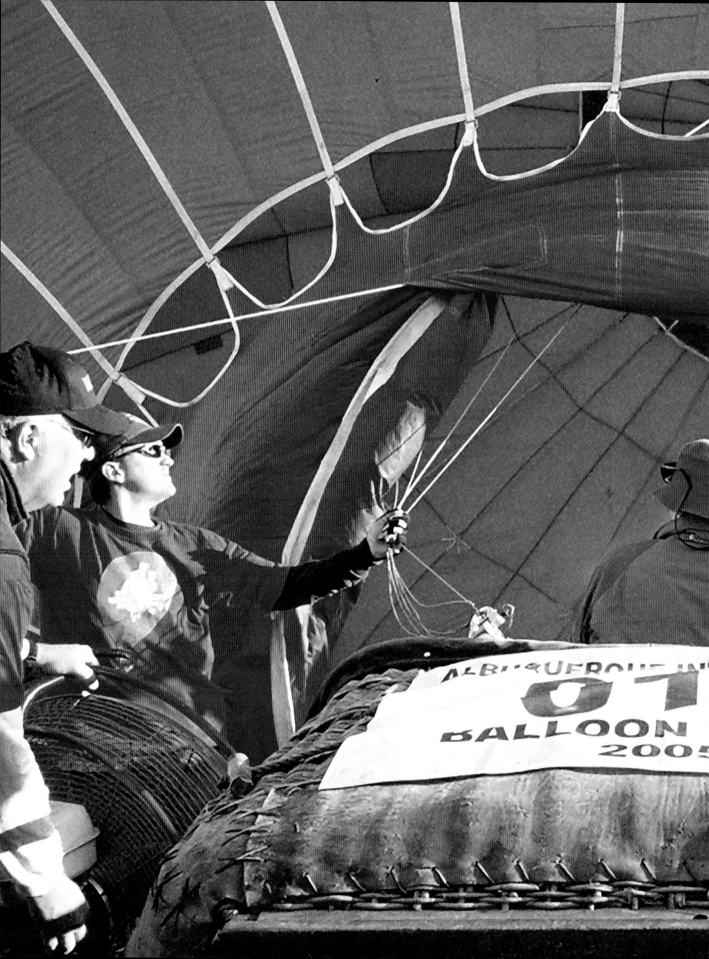

The Spirit of '76
and the Launching of AIBF

The year 1976 was the year of our nation's bicentennial celebrations and, across this great land of ours, there were many patriotic balloons in the air. And closer to home, Tom Rutherford chaired the Balloon Division of the Bicentennial Sports Alliance.

The Balloon Fiesta came under new management in 1976. Instead of an army of Albuquerque volunteers, a new non-profit corporation was created and a team of business professionals stepped forward to manage the fifth Albuquerque International Balloon Fiesta.

After four years of hard work and unbridled dedication in organizing and hosting this annual event, Sid Cutter and Tom Rutherford handed the reins over to the City of Albuquerque. The City then, under the able leadership of Mayor Harry Kinney, ballooning enthusiast extraordinaire, transferred responsibility to the newly formed Albuquerque International Balloon Fiesta, Inc. AIBF was created for a single purpose: to run the Fiesta like a business, including all organizational, financial and promotional aspects. Charlie Hines served as the first AIBF president and Betty Perkins, who worked tirelessly in transforming the volunteer committees of yesteryear into a well-run organization, served as AIBF chairwoman. The late Aubrey Cookman served as vice president and Sheri (Bachtell) Moore served as treasurer. In its first year of operation, AIBF hired Epstein Enterprises for marketing, advertising and public relations.

What else was going on back in 1976? Besides the American Revolution Bicentennial, Figure Skater Champion Dorothy Hamill won Olympic gold and the mini-series based on Alex Haley's "Roots" captivated TV viewers for weeks on end. Construction of the twin towers of the World Trade Center had just been completed. And in October, pilots and spectators arriving for the Balloon Fiesta initially found themselves upstaged by presidential politics as Jimmy Carter campaigned in Albuquerque. Back then, there was a supermarket chain known as Piggly Wiggly and for this Fiesta, AIBF had signed them up as a major sponsor.

Bob Ruppenthal was named the 1976 Balloonmeister and led a movement to put the fun back in balloon competition. Gone were the technical contests that so pre-occupied the 1973 and 1975 World Championships. If there was a need to resolve a pilot dispute, the score was settled by staging a light-hearted water balloon fight. Bob added southwestern flavors to Fiesta flying events. Roadrunner-Coyote chases substituted for traditional Hare-and-Hound races. While we have all seen New Mexico's state bird darting across a road and while we have all seen coyotes snooping around the city limits, has anyone really ever seen a pack of coyotes chase a roadrunner? Coyotes usually hunt alone but it did not matter. It just felt right to name the race after these two southwestern critters. Not to be forgotten was that prickly weed that tumbles along the ground when it is too windy to fly balloons. Our infamous tumbleweed took the place of fast-descending, weighted baggies. Local pilots snickered as they watched out-of-state pilots dis-

cover tumbleweeds to be one of the most aerodynamically inefficient projectiles ever dropped from a balloon. The 1976 Fiesta set the fun-filled pattern for all future Fiestas. In fact, it has been said at all subsequent Balloon Fiestas that the real winner is the pilot who has the most fun.

The 1976 Balloon Fiesta did not set any records in number of participating balloons (there were only about 140) but it did set a record in Fiesta weather. In looking back since the Fiesta's beginning, 1976 saw a morning record low temperature of 30 degrees. But this did little to cool spirits at Simms Field. The Fiesta saw nine consecutive, incident-free flying days, thanks to our good fortune in good flying weather, and in no small part to the diligence and skill of safety officers John Davis and Tim Thorsen, as well as launch directors JW Byrd, Bill and Frank Dickey, Brad Gibbs, Jim Harrington, Craig Landon and Ray Tillery.

And after all balloons landed safely, the fun continued on the ground. Those who were there remember an afternoon party sponsored by Rums of Puerto Rico and the Bud Man (alias Tom Rutherford) and his light-hearted antics at the final evening gala. And then there was the Busch Gardens film crew capturing the liftoff of 30 seemingly pilotless balloons for a special movie.

The formation of AIBF as a legal, non-profit entity in February 1976 greatly facilitated the recruiting of corporate sponsors, contributors and volunteers and instilled cooperation and community spirit, the necessary ingredients to assure that the fiesta would continue as an annual event to this very day. Calgary has its Stampede, New Orleans has its Mardi Gras, Pasadena has its Tournament of Roses Parade, Indianapolis has its Indy 500, and Albuquerque has its Balloon Fiesta. There is no doubt that the 1976 Balloon Fiesta bolstered Albuquerque's claim as the Balloon Capital of the World while putting the fun back in ballooning.

While America saluted its 200 years of independence, the Albuquerque Balloon Fiesta marked its first year of independence. With such an outpouring of support and commitment from the community, and the business management skills of the staff and volunteers of AIBF to make each fiesta a successful venture, the Spirit of '76 lives on from Balloon Fiesta to Balloon Fiesta.

❏ Dick Brown, 2003

Tips For Spectators

1. Keep your feet off the balloons.
2. Buy a program so you know what's up.
3. Bring lots of extra film.
4. Don't forget the camera.
5. Wear old warm clothes.
6. Wear comfortable "broken in" shoes or boots.
7. Keep your big feet off the balloons.
8. Work out before hand so you're in good shape.
9. Assist only when asked loudly by the pilot.
10. Get a full tank of gas before the race.
11. Keep one eye on the road and the other on the balloon.
12. And keep your grubby feet off the balloons.
13. Bring lots of money to buy the souvenirs.
14. When running after balloons, keep a sharp lookout for arroyos and rattlesnakes.
15. Don't harm the Roadrunners, they're our state bird.
16. Don't get caught speeding: you may spend the races in jail.
17. Please give the balloons the right of way.
18. Keep your pinkies off the balloons.
19. Bring more money on the second day for the rest of those souvenirs you've always wanted.
20. Don't smoke around the balloons especially when refueling.
21. Please don't drive thru the farmer's corn field.
22. Please don't knock down the fences.
23. Make sure your auto is insured and if you should have a wreck, please don't sue the balloon pilot (he's broke).
24. Bring your own champagne.
25. KEEP YOUR BIG FAT FEET OFF THE BEAUTIFUL BALLOONS!

❏ Sid Cutter, 1973 Official Fiesta Program

A Light in the Darkness: Dawn Patrol

On a cold October day in 1978, in the pre-dawn darkness, two California balloonists made history—and no doubt startled a few Albuquerque early risers – by ascending into the sunrise on the first flight ever of the Dawn Patrol. The flight was the culmination of six month's hard work and the realization of a dream, in the words of pilot Ron Thornton, "to be able to see the sunrise from a couple thousand feet above ground and see the morning shadows recede from above."

In 2002, the Dawn Patrol had its 25th celebration in Albuquerque. From a single pioneering flight by a couple of visionary pilots, the Dawn Patrol has become a tradition appreciated by spectators and balloonists alike. Balloon Fiesta visitors are delighted by the sight of the balloons ascending into the early morning dawn sky and majestically soaring over the still-shadowed field. Pilots watch the Dawn Patrollers closely and gratefully for a first indication of the winds they can expect when they ascend after sunrise.

When they came to the 1978 Albuquerque Balloon Fiesta, Thornton and Ken O'Connor had just received the certification from the Federal Aviation Administration that would permit them to fly their balloons at night. Balloons are generally certified to fly in daylight only for a very practical reason: the pilot needs to be able to see the ground, and obstacles on the ground, in order to be able to land safely. O'Connor and Thornton's idea was to take off at dawn and fly into daylight. By the time they were ready to land, they would be able to see buildings, power lines, and other obstructions on the ground.

In order to receive certification, O'Connor and

103

Thornton had to develop aircraft warning lights acceptable to the FAA and submit a ton of paperwork. They got the final OK just before they were to leave their home base in Morgan Hill, California for the Fiesta. Now, they were ready to set sail into the unknown.

Tom Christopher, now a Balloon Fiesta launch officer, writes: "I have the distinct honor of being the only passenger on this inaugural flight. It seems that Ron and Kenny needed an Albuquerque native to help maneuver in the skies over the city, [to help them know] where to go, and where to land. I fit the bill well, since I have been Kenny's chase crew chief and student pilot for the preceding two Fiestas.

"Soon we are inflating the balloon in the serene darkness of the mile high altitude of Albuquerque. As we complete our inflation, Ron and Ken pull out the new aircraft warning lights. They attach them to a nylon rope, which is attached to the gondola. The time is at hand, we heat the balloon and slowly ascend. Judy and Delores, our chase crew, hold the string of lights and turn them loose as we leave the dark parking lot.

"An added benefit to the sights available to the pilot, passengers and spectators is that when [the pilot heats] the balloon with its burners, the balloon lights up like a low watt light bulb, on a tremendous scale. When using the "fire 2" back up

fuel line on the balloon system, the glow increases tremendously and results are spectacular."

What Tom didn't describe is that incredible vista seen only by those lucky enough to fly the Dawn Patrol: the ground fading into oblivion under the balloon, pierced only by a glittering panorama of city lights, and the growing dawn, in shades of gray and pink and gold, breaking over the Sandia Mountains. Flying from the dark into the light is a beautiful and challenging experience.

2003 marked the 25th event anniversary of that very first Dawn Patrol flight. Ken O'Connor and Ron Thornton never dreamed how this wonder of the night would evolve. Over the years, the Dawn Patrol has grown and changed and slowly become an integral part of Fiesta. Today's Dawn Patrol includes two groups of balloonists. One group launches informally each day (weather permitting) from the northwest corner of the field. On mass ascension days beginning around 6 AM, another group performs the "Dawn Patrol Show," a synchronized inflation, launch, and flight set to narration and music.

Another well-loved tradition, the "balloon glow," also traces some of its roots back to those first Dawn Patrol flights. Before the Dawn Patrol came along, most balloonists had never seen the spectacular sight of a balloon in flight at night, lit softly from within by its burners. A mass nighttime ascension and flight would not have been practical. But eventually, a group of Albuquerque balloonists realized a static balloon display could be just as spectacular. That realization led to the creation of the first Luminaria Tour Balloon Display on Christmas Eve, 1979 in Albuquerque, a little more than a year after the first Dawn Patrol flight. Today, nighttime balloon displays are a staple at holiday and ballooning events around the world, and the

Albuquerque Fiesta's Balloon Glows rival the mass ascensions in attendance and popularity.

On the 25th anniversary of the Dawn Patrol, the ballooning community owes Ron Thornton and Ken O'Connor a great debt of gratitude, not only for getting the FAA to allow night flights, but for illuminating the dark morning skies with the magnificent glow of the Dawn Patrol overhead. Kenny is no longer with us—he passed away several years ago—but Ron Thornton is still flying, though on the other side of the country. He gets to Albuquerque for Fiesta once in awhile and still flies the Dawn Patrol.

And Tom Christopher writes, "Me, I am still a volunteer at the Fiesta. And I will always get goose pimples when I get to launch a Dawn Patrol flight."

❏ Kim Vesely, 2002

105

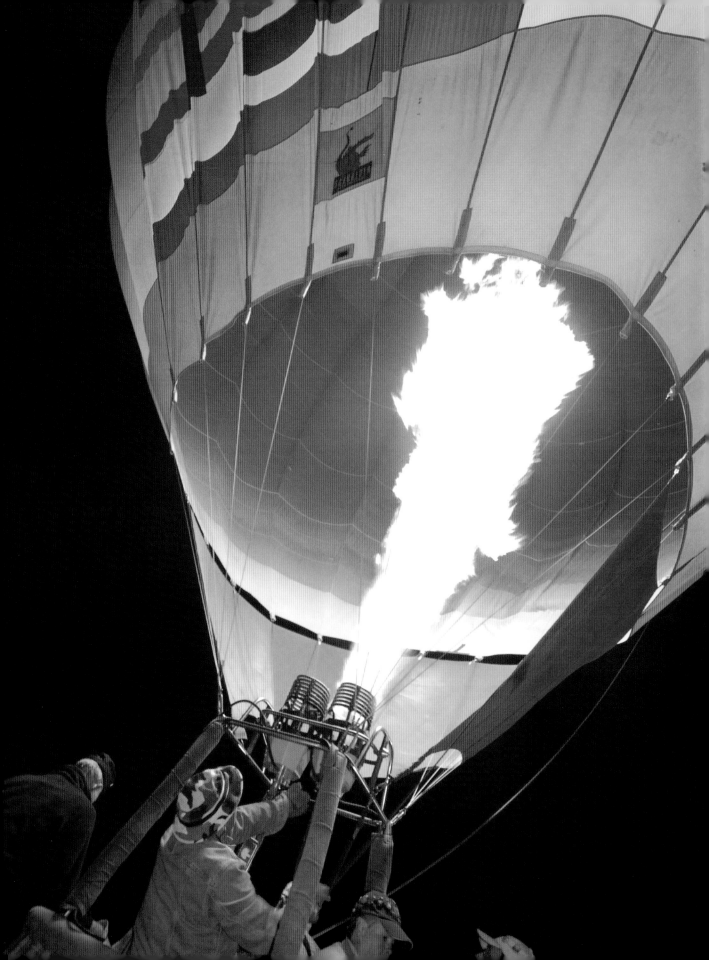

Balloon Glow:
The History

The Kodak Albuquerque International Balloon Fiesta Balloon Glow celebrates its 10th birthday in 1996. This awesome nighttime display of illuminated balloons has become one of the Fiesta's most popular events and is the largest display of its kind in the world.

The Balloon Glow was not invented by the Fiesta, but it was invented in Albuquerque. The idea that a nighttime balloon display could be a successful spectator event resulted from the inflation of a single balloon. Its pilot had just taken delivery and couldn't wait another minute to see what his new balloon looked like. The sight of the balloon lit from within its burner, glowing like a giant light bulb, awed the other balloonists who were on the scene. "Maybe other people would like to see this."

It was not the first time a balloon had been inflated at night—it had been done several times before, mostly for advertising purposes. But the idea of inflating several balloons together strictly as a nighttime display was totally new. The concept evolved into the first Luminaria Tour Balloon Display on Christmas Eve, 1979. After all, luminarias (properly called farolitos) are nothing but bags with candles inside, and a balloon is a great big colorful bag with a great big candle. Albuquerque's annual luminaria displays were already world-famous—balloons would be a natural addition. Most of all,

this display would give the balloonists the opportunity to say "thank you" to the citizens of Albuquerque who put up with them throughout the year.

Nineteen balloons, supported by dozens of ground crew, participated in the first display at the Albuquerque Country Club and the surrounding area. The sight of the colorful balloons, the flames from their burners flickering softly in the cold Christmas air, stunned even the balloonists them-

selves. An instant tradition had been created in the space of a few hours.

Meanwhile, word of the Albuquerque display was getting around through the balloonist grapevine. During the next few years, balloonists in communities worldwide created their own nighttime displays. One of them, Bill Bussey from Texas, coined the term "balloon glow" to describe the event. The name stuck.

In 1987, the Balloon Fiesta decided to hold a "balloon glow" to celebrate the 75th anniversary of New Mexico's statehood. Like everything else about the Fiesta, this would be the biggest event of its kind ever staged, with 250 balloons participating. At dusk Sunday evening, October 4, the forest of balloons stood erect, and via a live broadcast on KOB radio, Assistant Balloonmeister John Davis counted down the first "all burn." The concussion of light, heat and sound as all 250 balloons lit their burners and the huge crowd erupted in cheers blew away even the hardened Christmas Eve veterans. Many still get chills as they recall the thrill of that moment. As the sound faded, everyone knew that Fiesta had another success on its hands.

Technically, the Balloon Glow is not a difficult event for the balloonists. The "glow" effect is created by the same basic burner system used in flight. The balloons that light up the most brilliantly use various means to bypass the "pre-heat" coils on the burner. These coils help the burner work very efficiently, but the flame is a dull blue and does not throw a lot of light. When the coils are bypassed, the flame burns less efficiently but is a much brighter yellow. Several balloon manufacturers now offer a special "glow" option on their burners to create this effect, a demonstration of how far the night-time display of balloons has come since that cold Christmas Eve in 1979.

The Fiesta Balloon Glow has been a traditional first-weekend event every year since 1987, and in 1993 a "mini-glow" was added on the second weekend. Like all Balloon Fiesta events, the Balloon Glow is sensitive to wind and has to be cancelled if the winds blow too hard. However, the winds usually diminish in the evening, and the Balloon Glow has been "weathered out" only a few times over the years.

❑ Kim Vesely, 1996

Shaping Up
with Flying Colors

If you see pink elephants, you may not be high on J & B Whiskey. More likely, the Albuquerque Special Shapes Balloon Rodeo has turned on its fans.

113

The crowd loves the creative figures which portray unique objects. Some promote products like the 7-UP can, Safeway Grocery Cart or Ball Park Frank. Just about anything will fly: pigs, peacocks, peanuts.

In designs like *Chesty the Marine Bulldog* or *Mr. Snowman*, the round shape is obvious. In the *Cigarette Pack* or *Saguaro Cactus*, it isn't.

Ron Peterson, an Illinois minister, spent two years designing an ark complete with rainbow and 28 animals representing all continents. Immensely popular, *Arky* (see page 66) is one of the most complex balloons aloft. Each creature radiates a personality as it looks down and smiles. Aided by computers in the design and manufacturing process, Aerostar produced many of the little balloons (the critters) which pop up from the ark.

Another favorite balloon, the witch, evolved from a round black body with added stuff-lots of stuff. Spindly poison-green limbs dangle limply. Red boots protect her feet from the burner's heat. A spider wiggles in the wind. Her large green head with beak nose and black peaked hat work like a balloon on top of a balloon. On her back side, a cat hitches a ride on her broom.

Balloon Hilda, this wacky witch from Mitchell, South Dakota, lives at the balloon museum with her *Uncle Sam* and her friend *Chic-I-Boom*, a Carman Miranda lookalike. *Hilda* suggests they throw a Special Shapes Halloween party in Albuquerque. Using her cellular phone, she invites *Suleyman*, *Hagar* and others. *Uncle Sam* proposes hosting the shindig in the *Pink House*. *Hagar* wants the yellow cottage, but *Hilda* thinks the Disney castle will work best. She says, "It is haunted by dinosaurs and dragons."

They ask *Benihana*, who runs a restaurant, to plan the menu. He chooses Whoppers and a KFC bucket of chicken. *Beni* requests Smith's Grocery to send over a sack full of goodies. "Don't forget Kodak Film," someone shouts.

Sam and *Suley* take the truck to stock up on beverages. Korbel champagne, beer, Early Times whiskey, Pepsi, and Mountain Dew should do it. While flying home, a cop wearing a helmet and cruising on a Harley Davidson stops them, concerned about all that booze in the air. Suley says, "Hey, you're a balloon, come on along."

Back at the castle, relaxing in a blue recliner, *Santa* helps *Hilda* plan some entertainment. "A jack-o-lantern and Chinese bandit will add spooky ambiance," she says. "Let's ask ugly *Slick*, *Air-O-Gnat* and a *Smurf* to circulate and scare folks. And balloons, we'll need a bunch of balloons."

"We'll definitely bring a clown," says *Santa*. "I have one in my pack which we can fill with hot air."

Chici suggests games like, how many balloons can you stuff in a telephone booth or a tennis shoe?

"Balloonists love to play hare and hound," she says. "I'll ask Fred B. Rabbit and Aska dog to set it up."

"Let's bob for apples," *Hagar* adds. "And ask *Santa* to contribute a boom box and MTV."

Hilda requests everyone come as a favorite animal. Arky complains, "No way. I'm bringing my whole ark. I love them all."

The guests arrive by spaceship, yellow submarine, *Jumbo Jim's Plane*, and the *Santa Maria* ship. The cow comes by tractor.

Elephants and tigers and bears, oh my. *Miss Penny*, a pink pig, brings her brother *Li'l Buck*, then abandons him to flirt with a pig in a tux. She's in hog heaven. The stork stops by but can't stay; he has a baby to deliver. A polar bear and a penguin report to *Smokey Bear* that the only fires they've seen are from the burners of people flying balloons over the North Pole.

While *Garfield* and *Kit Kat* chase a macaw twice their size, the *Cheshire Cat* retreats from a flying Lab with her two pups.

Balloon Hilda swoops around the sky on her broom, bewitching everyone with her charm. The shapes party makes magic in the air. They all fly happily ever after.

If you spotted all 75 figures referred to above, you've probably been here before. Each has flown in Albuquerque. As these original creations rise with flying colors and meet up in ever-changing combinations, you can draft your own airy tale.

❑ Karen Yoor, 1995

115

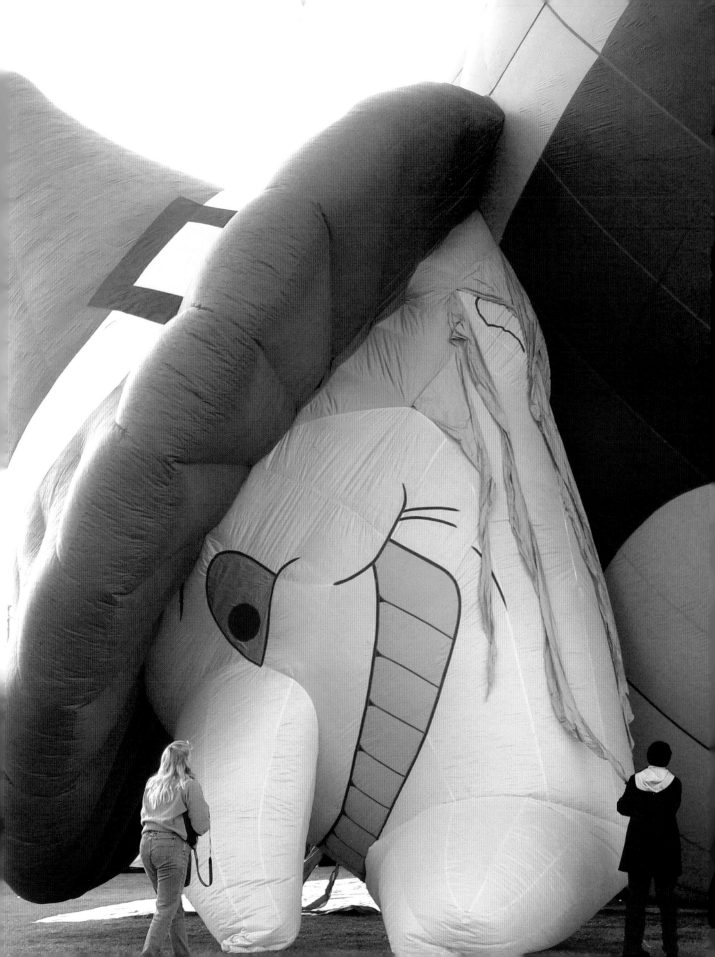

Fields of Color:
Fiesta Launch Sites Through the Years

In 1996, the Albuquerque International Balloon Fiesta moved to the sixth home in its 32-year history, a 360-acre facility. And for the first time, it's really a park. Balloon Fiesta Park doubles as a driving range and multi-use facility, and has a permanent clubhouse, restaurant, and oh, by the way, did you notice? GRASS on every launch site! The clouds of dust, which for 30 years were almost as much a part of Fiesta as the balloons, are a thing of the past. For the first time in its history, the Fiesta's home is truly spectator- and balloon-friendly.

Of course, in the beginning, nobody had any idea that Albuquerque would need a permanent facility (much less a grassed one) capable of supporting the world's biggest ballooning event. The Fiesta began as a one-time promotion to celebrate the 50th anniversary of KOB radio. The organizers had no idea what they were getting into!

Today, you can literally "shop 'till you drop" on the site of that first Balloon Fiesta. It was held on a big empty lot at the corner of San Pedro and Menaul, where the west end of Coronado Center is now located. (At the time, Coronado Center was much smaller and included the area between the present-day Mervyns [now Kohl's] and Sears stores).

As they say, the rest is history. More than 20,000 people showed up, and the resounding success of this 13-balloon event won Albuquerque the honor of hosting the First World Hot Air Balloon Championships in 1973. It was obvious a site was needed that could better accommodate the large crowds expected for a world-class event.

Albuquerque, fortunately, already had such a site: the racetrack at the State Fairgrounds. The infield area inside the track was plenty large to serve as a launch site, access to the launch field could be

123

What's the Largest Balloon Event?

On October 7, 2000, the *Albuquerque International Balloon Fiesta*® launched 329 hot air balloons in a one-hour period on opening day, earning a Guinness World Record.

restricted to pilots and crews, the track would make an ideal ground for the parades and other events, and fully-equipped grandstands could accommodate thousands of spectators. The 1973 World Championships and the 1974 Fiesta were held at the fairgrounds, as was the "transitional" rally in February 1975, the year Balloon Fiesta moved to October.

However, there were a couple of problems with the Fairgrounds. The new October date put the event right on the heels of the State Fair. Also, the Fairgrounds are (and were even in 1973) in the middle of one of the most congested areas in Albuquerque. Landing sites were a problem. Worse, any time the winds were out of the north—which, as regular Fiesta-goers know, is much of the time—the balloons went straight to the airport and Kirtland AFB. The stories of camera-toting international pilots landing inside the quadruple concertina-wire fences surrounding super-secret Manzano Base have long since passed into Fiesta legend.

So for the 1975 Balloon Fiesta and the second World Hot Air Balloon Championships, the event was on the move again. The new site was a cotton-wood-rimmed former alfalfa field owned by the Albert Simms family, located just northwest of what

is now the intersection of Jefferson and McLeod. The launch field was divided by earthen berms into 100' X 100' launch sites. Tents and trailers set up along the west end of the field provided souvenirs and snacks.

Simms Field, as it came to be known, proved to be a good location for a balloon launch site. At the time there was plenty of open land in the area where pilots could land and spectators could park. Best of all, pilots found that on this site they could take full advantage of the weather phenomenon that defines Fiesta among balloonists—the Albuquerque Box.

The Box occurs because cold air sinks overnight and flows down the Rio Grande Valley, creating wind that blows from the north to the south on and near the ground. However, the winds a few hundred feet off the ground often blow the opposite direction. Therefore, balloons can take off heading south, climb a few hundred feet and fly back north across the field, then drop down and end up close to where they took off. This degree of maneuverability is unusual, and word of the glories of "flying the Box" literally spread around the world. The great flying conditions, and the color and fun of Fiesta, made Albuquerque a place where balloonists wanted to fly.

With the move to Simms Field, the Balloon Fiesta was able to make one additional change that greatly increased the event's popularity and that of ballooning in general. For the first time, spectators were allowed onto the balloon launch sites. The experience of being actually on the field, surrounded by balloons and able to visit with crews and pilots proved truly magical. Over the years, hundreds of spectators whose first acquaintance with balloons was walking around the field at Fiesta have gone on to become balloonists themselves.

The Balloon Fiesta stayed at Simms Field for six years, from 1975 thru 1980. From the second year on, the concession area moved from the west side to the south and east side of the field, so spectators, shutterbugs, and film and TV cameras would not have to look into the sun while viewing the balloons. This orientation of infrastructure on the field was maintained with all the succeeding launch sites.

By 1980, developers had begun to build on Simms Field. In fact, in 1980, the Fiesta was able to use only the west half of Simms Field because construction had begun on the east end. It was high time to find another launch site. A more than suitable location was soon secured to the north and west of Simms Field, on land earmarked for gravel mining. This enormous site, which stretched from El Pueblo Rd. on the north to Osuna Blvd. on the south, was named Cutter Field, in honor of Albuquerque's first balloonist, Sid Cutter.

Cutter Field had more than enough room to house all of the Fiesta's parking and facilities, as well as a huge launch area that caused some to speculate the Balloon Fiesta might grow to 1,000 balloons.

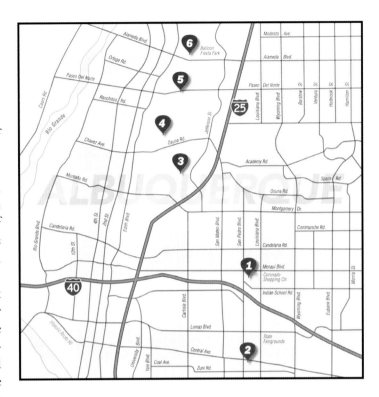

Balloon Fiesta locations
1. Coronado Shopping Center
   1972
2. State Fairgrounds
   1973-1974
3. Simms Field
   1975-1980
4. Cutter Field
   1981-1985
5. Balloon Fiesta Park #1
   1986-1995
6. Balloon Fiesta Park, permanent
   1996-present

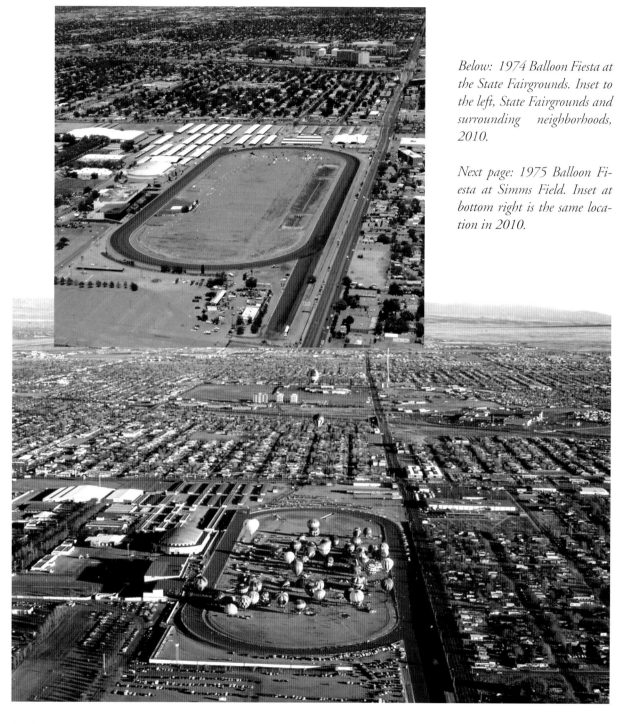

Below: 1974 Balloon Fiesta at the State Fairgrounds. Inset to the left, State Fairgrounds and surrounding neighborhoods, 2010.

Next page: 1975 Balloon Fiesta at Simms Field. Inset at bottom right is the same location in 2010.

Spectator parking was to the south of the launch site, and crew parking to the north. A propane refueling facility was installed at the very north end of the site—an important safety factor, since it permitted this facility to be isolated from the launch field and spectators.

The Balloon Fiesta flew from Cutter Field from 1981 through 1985. But after the 1985 Fiesta, gravel mining on the site had progressed far enough that the Fiesta could no longer use the site. Today, the area is being developed for single-family housing.

The Fiesta's next home, the first Balloon Fiesta Park, was originally a city landfill and was made safe and available for the Fiesta's use by the city of Albuquerque. It stretched along a narrow corridor of land south of Alameda Blvd. It was as compact as Cutter Field had been large—just 77 acres, bordered on the east by high power lines which made it necessary to launch balloons only from the western side of the site. By assigning four or five balloons to a launch square, the site could accommodate 500 or so balloons, but it was close quarters. The Fiesta worked with neighboring landowners to accommodate parking and RV sites, and Sandia Pueblo agreed to allow the Fiesta to move its propane facility onto tribal land off north Edith Blvd.

For the first time, the Balloon Fiesta was able to install some permanent infrastructure, including roads and power to supply the growing number of concessions, hospitality suites, and official facilities. The non-profit corporation that runs the Balloon Fiesta built its first permanent headquarters near the field. But the site's limitations were stifling. It was simply too small to permit the Fiesta to grow, and the search began for another site. The old Fiesta Park is now used for RV and spectator parking and as a target site for balloon competition.

The Balloon Fiesta's current field was originally, like Cutter Field, a gravel mining site. Balloonists were very familiar with it, because many of them launched out of this "north gravel pit" to fly to the old Fiesta Park for key grab and other events. The city of Albuquerque and the state of New Mexico acquired this site for development as a multi-use park and a permanent home for the Balloon Fiesta. In 1996, the Albuquerque International Balloon Fiesta celebrated its 25th event at its new, and current, site. Though as many as 1,000 balloons (in 2000) have participated, the event's size has now settled at around 750 balloons. Neighboring landowners, and Sandia Pueblo just to the north, have been very helpful in facilitating parking and balloon flights.

Since 1996, the city of Albuquerque, the Balloon Fiesta, and private developers have continued to improve Balloon Fiesta Park (did we mention the grass?). And there's more to come. At the 2002 Fiesta, ground was broken for the Anderson-Abruzzo Albuquerque International Balloon Museum adjoining Balloon Fiesta Park. The museum opened in 2005, providing a year-round presence at Balloon Fiesta Park. After a long march north, Albuquerque now can boast a facility truly worthy of the world's biggest ballooning event.

❏ Kim Vesely, 2003

Around the World in 13,700 Days

While the Albuquerque International Balloon Fiesta plays out in US airspace, it involves far more than one nation. From its earliest beginnings, the Balloon Fiesta has been a gathering of different nations.

In a way, the Balloon Fiesta has gone global, but not in the sense of global warming or global economy. Instead it is global in nature, meaning pilots participating in friendly balloon competition see themselves as collectively representing "one world" while proudly representing their individual countries. Sid Cutter's World Balloon is a great symbol of political divisions being overcome by sporting competition. So just how "international" has the Balloon Fiesta been over the years?

One way to answer this is to look at the steady growth of international pilots and hot air balloons participating over the years. The 1972 event, a Roadrunner-Coyote Balloon Race, led directly to the first world competition, and ever since then, the Balloon Fiesta has been multi-national. In 1973, 15 nations, including **Denmark**, **Ireland**, **Norway, Switzerland** and **France** (whose Mont-golphiere brothers invented the hot air balloon), competed in the First World Hot Air Balloon Championships. Who can ever forget the excitement and intrigue of having Veikko Kaseva of **Finland**, with his homebuilt balloon, and 72-year-old Franco Segre of **Italy**, at the time the oldest hot air balloon pilot in the world, on the launch field?

The only international pilot to finish in the top group, in a race dominated by Americans, was Janne Balkedal of **Sweden**. In a gesture of Southwestern hospitality that has continued to present-day, Albuquerque residents have not only welcomed international pilots to the city, but have taken them into their homes.

The first world gathering was such a great milestone in international hot air ballooning that the US Postal Service honored the event by issuing a 15-cent aerogramme (see next page), with the first day ceremony for this balloon-design postal souvenir in Albuquerque.

Franco Segre, the oldest hot air balloon pilot in the world in 1973

The 1974 Balloon Fiesta saw only six nations take to the sky, but the next year, there were 16 as the event was held in conjunction with the Second World Hot Air Balloon Championships. Balkedal of Sweden finished second, with Peter Vizzard of **Australia** third, and the three competitors from the

131

Buffalo Chip Chapter of the Dublin Balloon Club, 1974

United Kingdom (Peter Hall, Dick Wirth and Martin Moroney) close behind.

The number of participating nations dropped to three in 1976 as the United States celebrated its Bicentennial, and back then we welcomed Jesus Gonzalez-Green of Madrid, **Spain** to Albuquerque. We almost missed making that international claim in 1977 and 1978 (and also in 1983), but Tatsuo Fujimori of Tokyo, **Japan**; Phil Hutchins of the **United Kingdom**; and Jim Grosset of Calgary, **Canada**; respectively, came through as the only non-USA participants, and thus kept our international claim alive. During the period 1979-1991, the number of international balloons in the Balloon Fiesta numbered less than ten per year. But we had several first time nations join us, includ-

ing Iain Cave and Jeannette Van Ginkle of **South Africa** in 1981; Vishwa Gupta of New Delhi, **India** in 1985; and Gintarus Surkus of Kaunas, Lithuania, **USSR** in 1989.

The number of international balloons increased to 11 in 1992 and stayed at that level for three years straight. During this period, we met A'Kos Horvath of Budapest, **Hungary** and Joe Gilles of Naranjo, **Costa Rica**. Then in 1995, Antonio Marques of Sao Paulo, **Brazil** and Gunars Dukste of Riga, **Latvia** helped us reach a count of 13 nations. In 1996, we reached 16, the most international pilots since the Second World Championships. That's when we met Jana Bartosova and Jan Smrcka of Prague, **Czech Republic** and Roman Godlewski of Bialystok, **Poland**.

The 1997 Balloon Fiesta saw a surge in the number of participating countries with 24, including six first-timers. Antonio Lopes Da Silva of Lisboa, **Portugal**; Milomie Stoskovic of Beograd (Belgrade), **Yugoslavia**; Tom Miklousic of Lagreb, **Croatia**; Ismail Keremoglu of Mimlar Sitasi Batiken, **Turkey**; Slavko Sorn of Ljubljana, **Slovenia**; and Carlos Hermann of Ituzaingo, **Argentina** all came to Albuquerque. In 1998 there were 16 nations, including Sergio Rios of Caracas, **Venezuela** and in 1999 there were 18 nations, including Joe Brown of Nairobi, **Kenya** and Gael Cardon de Lichtbuer of Funglinster, **Luxembourg**.

The all-time high came in 2000 when 26 nations converged on Balloon Fiesta Park. These included several new countries—Jon and Cherie Hanley of **Malaysia**; Marco Rodriguez of **Mexico**; Alexandre Firsakov of **Belarus**; Shai Shelhav of **Israel**; Tariq al Omari of **Jordan**; and Manzoor Bajwa of **Pakistan**. The Balloon Fiesta has averaged 20 countries

INTERNATIONAL HOT AIR BALLOONING • AEROGRAMME • VIA AIRMAIL • PAR AVION

per year ever since.

Joining 20 other nations for the 30th Balloon Fiesta in 2001 were Robertas Komza of Vilnius, **Lithuania** and Tariq al Omari again, this time from Abu Dhabi, **United Arab Emirates**. In 2002, there were 23 nations, including Jae Song of Seoul, **South Korea**; Miroslav Mocary of Kosice, **Slovakia Republic**; and Karol Slabak of Podbrezova, also in Slovakia. The next year, Vladimir Karnaukhov of Feodosia, **Ukraine** joined 23 other international pilots. There were 16 nations at the 2004 Balloon Fiesta and the same again in 2005. That was the year when the Anderson-Abruzzo Albuquerque International Balloon Museum first opened its doors at Balloon Fiesta Park. In full spirit of international unity, the museum features one of the finest collections of historic balloons and ballooning artifacts in the world.

More than anything else, the "Flight of the Nations" has exemplified the international spirit and global outreach of the Balloon Fiesta. It started in 1997 when 40 nations were invited to send one pilot to carry the flag for his/her country, thus recognizing their international contribution to the Balloon Fiesta. Ever since then, the Wednesday morning "Flight of the Nations" mass ascension has created high anticipation among organizers, spectators and frequent flyers, anxious to welcome new nations participating for the first time. In 2006 and 2007, the Flight of the Nations featured 19 countries.

In 2008, there were 23 nations and last year there were 18, including 20 international special shape balloons. When it comes to the Special Shapes Rodeo, 28 nations have participated to date but none more enthusiastically than Brazil which has brought ten special shapes to the Balloon Fiesta

Commander Mark Prokopius, Commanding Officer of USS New Mexico, describes his submarine's global reach and peace-keeping missions to KOAT-TV co-anchors Melissa Montoya and Marisa Maes

Visitors from around the world come to Balloon Fiesta each year, including this group of students from Annonay, France, the original home town of Joseph-Michel and Jacques-Étienne Mongolfier and the site of the Montgolfier brother's first public unmanned hot air balloon flight.

133

during each of the past two years. Besides the USA and Canada, other consistent rodeo participants include **Belgium** and **Germany**. In recent years, many of the Balloon Fiesta's best-known special shapes have been built in Brazil and Belgium.

A story about international participation at the Albuquerque International Balloon Fiesta would not be complete without mention of the concurrent gas ballooning events at Balloon Fiesta Park. These include four Coupe Gordon Bennett balloon races with anywhere from six to twelve nations competing, including **Austria** and **Netherlands**, the 9th World Gas Balloon Championships in 1994 with seven nations, and 13 America's Challenge gas balloon races, the first being in 1995.

In the 38 years of Balloon Fiesta events, balloonists have come from Australia and the South Seas, including Malaysia as well as **Macau**, **New Zealand** and **Singapore**. From South America, Argentina, Brazil and Venezuela have helped reinforce international friendships. Bringing new connec-

tions from a distant mystical part of the world are Kenya and South Africa. Israel, Jordan and UAE have represented the Mid-East. India, Pakistan, Japan and South Korea have brought cultural greetings from afar. From the former states of the USSR, Latvia, Lithuania, Belarus and Ukraine have graced fiesta skies, and there is great pleasure seeing the smiling pilot faces of **Russia** ascending from the balloon field, a show of optimism in the endless quest for global peace.

The Albuquerque International Balloon Fiesta has grown into a celebration of global friendship and peace. Just look at the tally of European nations: Ireland, United Kingdom, Portugal, Spain, France, Belgium, Luxembourg, Netherlands, Germany, Switzerland, Italy, Austria, Slovenia, Croatia, Yugoslovia, Turkey, Hungary, Slovakia Republic, Czech Republic, Poland, Denmark, Norway, Sweden and Finland—all have helped make the Balloon Fiesta truly international. And from Central America and North America, Costa Rica, Mexico and Canada have joined the United States in representing the international ballooning community.

All told, that's 49 of 196 nations that have flown Albuquerque skies. In other words, 25% of the countries in the world have participated in the Albuquerque International Balloon Fiesta. From the day of the first Albuquerque hot air ballooning event on April 8, 1972 to the final day of last year's Balloon Fiesta, that is, October 11, 2009, we have gone around the world in 13,700 days! And during that time, international pilots have represented "one world" where magical balloon journeys abound and where buoyant flight inspires imagination. As Disney would say, it's a small world after all.

❏ Dick Brown, 2010

134

Opposite page: 2005 America's Challenge. Above: The 2010 America's Challenge is ready to launch

Albuquerque's Golden Age & Revival of Distance Gas Ballooning

Once upon a time, the only way to get anywhere in the air was by balloon. From the 1783 discovery that hot air or a lighter-than-air gas captured in a big bag could propel a basketful of humans aloft to the beginning of powered flight in 1906, balloons were the only form of flight. Balloon exhibitions dazzled everyone from kings (one of the first was at Versailles) to common county fairgoers. Those magnificent men, and more than a few women, in their flying machines were larger than life figures and many lived larger than life lives.

Ed Yost

Eventually, there was even a balloon race: the Coupe Aéronautique Gordon Bennett, founded by American expatriate newspaperman James Gordon Bennett in 1906. The challenge: to fly the longest distance from the starting point. These difficult and dangerous races—remember, weather forecasting then wasn't what it is now—continued up until the beginning of World War II. By then, the airplane was the hot new machine and the romantic aura that surrounded balloonists had mostly shifted to daring early aviators. World War II hastened the further development of the airplane and air travel, both for warlike and peaceful purposes.

Above all, airplanes could get people to a set destination with some degree of certainty, whereas with balloons you could only get from point A to point B if the wind was blowing that way. So after the war, ballooning all but disappeared from the scene. The Gordon Bennett race was not revived, the modern hot air balloon had yet to be invented, and only a few adventurers and gas balloon enthusiasts kept the first form of flight aloft.

Ballooning began to see a sort of renaissance with the development of the propane burner in 1960, which made hot air ballooning practical and relatively affordable. Balloon events and even "races" began to crop up, including (in 1972) the Albuquerque International Balloon Fiesta. But hot air events were pretty much strictly local affairs. Hot air balloon flights typically lasted an hour or two and balloons usually landed within a few miles of the takeoff point. Gas flights still occurred, notably in Europe where the availability of cheap hydrogen made the sport affordable and practical. But even those flights were relatively local in nature. Gas balloon competitions, like hot air competitions, involved flying to a specified target. While these targets were further away and the flights were longer—a day or two, since gas balloons could stay aloft longer—they generally covered only a few hundred miles.

The Transatlantic Challenge

Throughout, there were always adventurers: aeronauts who pushed the boundaries and tried to fly higher, longer, and farther than ever before. For these adventurers, the ultimate challenge was to cross the Atlantic Ocean. The flight was first tried in the mid-1800s. By the mid 1970s, nearly a dozen attempts had been made, including one notable flight from east to west. Always, fickle winds and the daunting expanse of ocean had stymied would-be conquerors. Five people died in the attempt, swallowed up without a trace by the unrelenting sea.

In 1976, the remarkable Ed Yost took up the challenge, flying alone in a silver and black balloon over a fiberglass catamaran-style gondola called the *Silver Fox*. Yost, generally regarded as the father of modern hot-air ballooning, had invented the propane-fired balloon burner in the early 1960s. With Don Piccard, Yost had made the first hot air balloon crossing of the English Channel in the early 1960s, sitting on a gondola that was literally a piece of plywood. In other words, the guy had guts.

Yost didn't make it—he landed safely near the

Azores—but his flight convinced others that the Atlantic might be crossable. One of these adventurers was Maxie Anderson, an Albuquerque businessman who was one of the first balloonists in a city of balloonists. Anderson read about Yost's flight in *National Geographic* and was captured by the romance and adventure of the challenge. With his friend and fellow Albuquerquean Ben Abruzzo, he contracted with Yost to build the *Double Eagle*, named in honor of the Lone Eagle, Charles Lindbergh, who made the first airplane crossing of the Atlantic in 1927. Lindbergh had landed at Le Bourget Airport in Paris, and Le Bourget became the goal and the grail.

Abruzzo and Anderson launched their first attempt in September 1977 from Marshfield, Massachusetts. They soon were caught in a huge low-pressure system that literally flew them in circles in some of the worst weather balloonists have ever survived. They finally ended the flight just off the coast of Iceland, chastened, frozen, but alive. Ben's first reaction: "I'll never do this again."

But a couple of months in sunnier, warmer Albuquerque revived Ben's spirits and Ben and Maxie began to plan a second attempt using a larger balloon, *Double Eagle II*. With a third partner, Larry Newman, they set off from Presque Isle, Maine in August 1978. Their epic flight set a duration record for gas balloons that still stands and ended successfully just a few miles short of Le Bourget.

During the same period, other balloonists had made credible attempts, including Colorado's Dewey Reinhard and—most notably—Britain's Don Cameron and Christopher Davey, who almost beat *Double Eagle II* across the Atlantic. These events excited media interest, but nothing like the

Abruzzo and Anderson in Iceland after being plucked from the ocean in September 1977

press frenzy that accompanied the success of the *Double Eagle II*. The landing was the lead story on all the network newscasts, front-page news in papers worldwide, and made the covers of many major newsmagazines. The world was in need of some good news, and the Albuquerque trio delivered.

It was all in all a glorious time for ballooning in Albuquerque. Sid Cutter had just won the national hot-air balloon championship. Paul Woessner, then living in Albuquerque, was the reigning world hot air balloon champion and would win the title again in 1979. The Balloon Fiesta's draw as an international event was strong, and Albuquerque was in every way the "balloon capital of the world."

Going the Distance

The success of the *Double Eagle II* both as an adventure and as a media event excited a renewed interest in long-distance balloon flight. Some of this manifested itself in further attempts to conquer oceans and continents. Maxie Anderson and his son Kris made the first non-stop flight across North America in 1980. In 1981, Ben Abruzzo

Maxie and Kris Anderson's Kitty Hawk *preparing to launch near the Golden Gate Bridge for its flight across North America in May 1980*

and Larry Newman, with Ron Clark and Rocky Aoki, successfully spanned the Pacific Ocean in the *Double Eagle V*. Soon after, Anderson and fellow balloonist Don Ida crossed the Indian Ocean on the first of three attempts to fly around the world. However, completion of the around-the-world challenge had to await the refinement of other ballooning technologies, especially that of the "Rozier" balloon, a hybrid of gas and hot-air originally invented in 1783. It was not until 1999 that the non-stop around-the-world challenge was met, by Bertrand Piccard and Brian Jones in the *Breitling Orbiter III*.

Meanwhile, others remembered that high adventure need not be limited to crossing continents and oceans. The idea of a "race" across the Atlantic Ocean had been floated by Abruzzo and Anderson as early as the aftermath of their first transatlantic attempt. While that idea proved somewhat impractical at the time (there finally was such a race in

1992), there already was a precedent for something just as exciting, but shorter and less expensive: the Coupe Gordon Bennett model abandoned with World War II.

In 1979, promoter and balloon enthusiast Tom Heinsheimer found there was considerable interest among the world's handful of gas balloonists in a distance race. This spectacular event, featuring nearly two dozen balloons from all over the world, launched from a suitably romantic '30s-era setting: the dock next to the *Queen Mary* in Long Beach, California. The object: fly further than anybody else. The weather didn't cooperate, the balloons got into the Los Angeles airport traffic pattern (oops!), and the eventual winners (Abruzzo and Anderson, in *Double Eagle III*), spent a day over the ocean before swinging back over land and ending up in southwestern Colorado—a short flight by today's distance-ballooning standards.

Despite these and other controversies, the race had proved that gas balloon distance races could be exciting events and that there was still an appetite among balloonists and the public for going the distance. Heinsheimer eventually promoted several additional races. Then, in 1983, the ballooning division of the International Aeronautics Federation (Fédération Aéronautique Internationale, or FAI for short) re-founded the Coupe Gordon Bennett. The race has been held every year since then except for two years when it had to be cancelled due to unfavorable weather and airspace conditions.

Which Brings Us Back to Albuquerque . . .

Gas balloon races were a part of the Albuquerque International Balloon Fiesta throughout much

Coupe Gordon Bennett

In 1906, spectators gathered in Paris' famed Tuilières Gardens, in the shadow of the Louvre, to cheer on the competitors in history's first air race. Newspaper entrepreneur James Gordon Bennett, Jr., an American newspaper publisher living in France, sponsored the race that still bears his name, the Coupe Aéronautique Gordon Bennett. An American team, Frank Lahm and Henry Hersey, flew to victory, traveling nearly 400 miles (641 km). Their victory brought the race to the United States for the first time.

Since then, 28 cities in seven nations have had the honor of hosting a Gordon Bennett. Only three cities have hosted the race more than three times: Brussels, Belgium; Paris, France; and Albuquerque, USA.

By tradition, the home country of the team that wins the race is afforded the honor of hosting the event the next year (recently changed to two years later). In 1993 and 2005, Albuquerque became the host city after American teams won the previous year's Gordon Bennett (David Levin and James Herschend in 1992; Richard Abruzzo and Carol Rymer Davis in 2004). But in 1998 and 2007, there was no Gordon Bennett winner because the race was cancelled. So in those years, the world air sports governing body, the Fédération Aéronautique Internationale, solicited bids from cities wishing to host the Gordon Bennett, and both times, Albuquerque was chosen to host the next year's race, in 1999 and 2008.

of the 1980s. These races, like hot air balloon events and the World Gas Championships, involved precision flying to a target. Distance was not the objective, though the targets were generally in eastern New Mexico or west Texas, a considerable distance from the launch site. Eventually, interest in participating in these races waned, and the gas balloon races disappeared for a time.

In 1993, however, a new opportunity arose: the chance to host the Coupe Aéronautique Gordon Bennett. The previous year, the race had been won by American David Levin, a Coloradoan very familiar with the Balloon Fiesta. By virtue of his win, the U.S. had the right to host the next Gordon Bennett, and Albuquerque was chosen as the site. The event proved to be such a success that the next year the Albuquerque Balloon Fiesta became

the site for the World Gas Balloon Championships, a series of competitive "tasks" flown to targets. But no such international event was slated for Albuquerque in 1995.

Into the breach stepped Mark Sullivan, an Albuquerque balloonist and member of the Balloon Fiesta board who was an experienced gas balloonist. Mark proposed that the Balloon Fiesta create its own event: the America's Challenge for gas balloons. Like the Gordon Bennett, it would be a distance race and would take advantage of the possibility of long flights across the North American continent with a minimum of international airspace issues (just one international border, Canada, routinely comes into play).

American and international pilots jumped at the chance to compete in another prestigious distance

Spectators get ready for the launch of the 2008 America's Challenge

race. Some fourteen contestants from five countries showed up for the first race, won by Richard Abruzzo and Dave Melton. They flew nearly 1,400 miles, a formidable distance by any standard. The race has been held every year since except for 1999 and 2009. In 1999, the race was suspended so Albuquerque could host the Gordon Bennett that year (the America's Challenge has been held in Albuquerque concurrently with the Gordon Bennett twice since, in 2005 and 2008). The 2009 race was cancelled due to high winds. The America's Challenge routinely attracts around a dozen pilots hungry for adventure coupled with the beauty of floating high above the American landscape.

❑ Kim Vesely, 2009

Dame Blanche *launches as the Hare balloon in the first Balloon Fiesta gas balloon race, 1981*

Early Fiesta Gas Ballooning

The Albuquerque International Balloon Fiesta is known principally as a hot air balloon event. However, in recent years its long-distance gas balloon races have gained growing fame, prestige, and popularity. Although the America's Challenge race for gas balloons is a relatively new event, gas balloon races and exhibitions have been a part of the Balloon Fiesta almost since its beginning.

Carol Rymer Davis (center) and her crew prepare to launch in the 1982 race

The first Balloon Fiesta gas flight was made in the event's second year, in 1973, at the end of the First World Championships. Ed Yost, the Clerk of the Course for the Championships (the rough equivalent of Balloonmeister), made a gas balloon flight on the final Sunday. Ed had brought a polyethylene balloon with him and offered rides to six other people for $1,000 apiece. After a flight from the State Fairgrounds – at that time, the Balloon Fiesta's launch site—the balloon envelope was cut up into pieces and sold to the spectators for $ .50 each. In 1975, during the Second World Championships, German aeronaut "Jo Jo" Maes flew a gas balloon from the Simms' Field launch site.

After that, the Balloon Fiesta took a break from gas ballooning until October of 1981. With a resurgence of gas balloon flying in the US, the Balloon Fiesta decided to sponsor a gas balloon race that would be part of the BFA National Championship Series. The competition, a Hare and Hound, was scheduled to take off on Tuesday, 6 October, but was delayed by weather until Wednesday. That afternoon 16 balloons followed the Hare balloon,

Dame Blanche, piloted by Event Director John Davis, Carol Rymer Davis and Scoring Officer Nick Saum. The goal of the competition was to land as close to the Hare balloon as possible. After a fourteen-hour flight, the Hare landed near Ulysses, Kansas. The winning balloon *Chicago*, piloted by Dean Stellas and John Rippenger, landed seven miles away.

The landings were interesting, and there was some excitement during the takeoff when the balloon flown by Maxie Anderson and Don Ida tried to fly through the balloon of Herb Wilcox and Fred Hyde. No harm was done and both balloons were able to fly.

The 1982 race, again a BFA sanctioned event, allowed the pilots to pick one of four targets: Clayton and Glenrio in New Mexico and Littlefield and Amarillo in Texas. There were only eleven balloons entered because the Balloon Fiesta immediately followed the Gas World Championships which had been held in Switzerland. The race ended with the teams of Herb Wilcox and Fred Hyde and John Shoecraft and Fred Gorrell tied for 1st. Both balloons landed 2.3 miles from the Clayton Airport. Of note was the last place flight of Nikki Caplan and Jane Buckles who landed in Iowa, setting a women's world record for distance.

The 1983 event was again a part of the BFA National Championship Series. This race consisted of a Race to a Line and a Race to a Point. The lines were state boundaries and the points were towns on or very near these lines. Fourteen balloons took off on Sunday, 3 October, from Cutter Field and landed in New Mexico, Texas, Oklahoma and Kansas. The winner was John Shoecraft who landed in Texola, Oklahoma.

Dame Blanche *being inflated for the 1982 race*

With four US balloons in Zurich competing in the prestigious Coupe Gordon Bennett, the 1984 race had only three entries. The BFA task for the balloons was a Judge Declared Goal. After a delay because officials were worried that the balloons might fly into White Sands Missile Range the balloons took off on Monday, 8 October. The winner was the team of Jim Schiller and Randy Woods, with a landing near Borger, Texas.

Weather became the chief feature of the 1985 race. The five balloons were to compete in the now familiar Race to a Line and Race to a Goal. Shortly after takeoff they all encountered snow which add-ed to the complexity of the flight. There were some interesting landings including one on the side of Pecos Baldy. There were no injuries, but some pi-lots came back with great stories. The winner was the late Fred Hyde, with a landing near Elliott, Kansas.

Weather again played havoc with the 1986 race. By the time the race took place on Tuesday morn-ing the entry list was down to five balloons who were to compete in a Multiple Judge Declared Goal and Distance event. The winners were Jaques Sou-kup and Mark Sullivan with a flight to Galisteo, New Mexico.

Launch time approaches for the 1982 race

The seventh and last of the early AIBF Gas Balloon Races took place on 8 October, 1987. Again, the Gordon Bennett, scheduled at the same time in Austria, siphoned off many potential competitors. Only one balloon flew, and George Hahn was awarded 3rd place for that flight.

With the rising expense of flying gas balloons and no sponsor in sight, the Balloon Fiesta Board of Directors decided to discontinue the annual Gas Balloon Race. It would not be until the 1990's that gas ballooning returned to the Balloon Fiesta. In 1993, Albuquerque and Balloon Fiesta played host to the Coupe Gordon Bennett, and in 1994 to the World Gas Balloon Championships. Both are long-distance events, where the winners are the team that flies the longest distance from the launch point. The success of these events inspired the creation of the Balloon Fiesta's own gas balloon distance race—the America's Challenge.

❏ John Davis, 2004

Officials Make Safe Flights

Hot air balloon flying events are under the direction of the Balloonmeister, who is the chief official in charge of flight operations. The Balloonmeister is an experienced balloonist and Balloon Fiesta veteran who usually has worked his/her way up through the officials' ranks and has participated in Balloon Fiesta for many years both as an official and as a pilot. All but one of the 22 Balloonmeisters in the event's 39-year history have been from the Albuquerque metro area, and four have been women (called Balloonmeisterin). The Balloonmeister oversees all of the officials responsible for flight operations and works with the Executive team and the chief officials to determine if weather conditions will allow for safe flights. The Balloonmeister customarily—but not always—serves for two or three years.

The Balloonmeister is assisted by the Assistant Balloonmeister, who assists with all aspects of flight operations. While some have likened the job to being Vice-President, the Assistant Balloonmeister is kept plenty busy, and often oversees some of the flying events and especially "grounded" events like Balloon Glows. The Assistant Balloonmeister often—but not always—moves up to the Balloonmeister slot.

Reporting to the Balloonmeister are the Safety, Launch, and Scoring operations. The Chief Safety Official and his/her team of ten Safety Officials

are responsible for assuring pilots follow the rules and regulations governing the Balloon Fiesta and, when necessary, discussing safety issues with pilots. If necessary, the Safety Team with the support of the Balloonmeister can ground pilots who violate rules. The Safety Team also assists with accident investigations, landowner relations, and works with Federal Aviation Administration officials to promote a safe and fun event. Safety Officials are experienced balloonists, many of whom have served in other areas of flight operations before moving to Safety.

The most visible officials on the field, in their black-and-white striped attire, are the "Zebras," more properly called Launch Directors. Launch Directors essentially function as traffic control officers, controlling the pace and safety of balloon inflations and launches. They advise pilots when they can begin inflation, "go hot" (stand the balloon upright), and finally provide a final check of balloon traffic in the area and give pilots the "thumbs up" to launch. The Launch Directors also assist with guest safety and crowd control to keep people out of

What's with all the stripes?

All those referees in black and white are not throwing yellow flags—they're actually the launch directors or zebras for all the balloons. The zebras perfom a vital task: helping balloons to launch safely in the midst of hundreds of thousands of people milling around. As weather conditions change and balloon crews experience unexpected situations, these directors provide valuable advice and decisions on whether or not a balloon may launch. If you hear a whistle blowing and see a zebra giving "thumbs up," look up because a balloon is taking off.

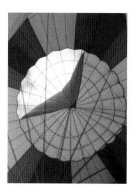

the way of balloons launching and landing.

With their colorful costumes—this is one fun-loving group!—the Zebras are also perhaps the Balloon Fiesta's most visible ambassadors. They need to know the answers to everything from the location of the nearest porta-pottie to the best places to go for breakfast burritos, because somebody is going to ask. Most Launch Directors are balloon pilots or experienced crew members; many have been Zebras for 20 years or more. There are even second-generation Launch Directors, as sons and daughters follow their parents in donning the black and whites.

The third large group of officials are the Scoring Officers under the supervision of the Chief Scoring Official and Assistant Chief Scoring Official. The scoring operation is divided into two areas: targets and operations. The target group (about 25 Scoring Officials), under the supervision of the Chief and Assistant Chief Target Officials, is responsible for setting out the targets (or erecting the poles), watching approaching balloons to make sure they are flying safely and in accordance with the competition rules (and reporting issues to the Safety team as necessary), and measuring the distance each marker is dropped to the target. The target group then turns its data over to the operations group, which is responsible for crunching the numbers and reporting the results.

The officials' day doesn't end until every balloon has safely landed. Their chief satisfaction comes from a "clean" day—no accidents or serious incidents, a day of safe flights and soft landings.

❏ Kim Vesely, 2011

THE BALLOON FIESTA THAT ALMOST WASN'T

"As a result of today's tragic events that have impacted our country, we have received numerous calls about the status of the 2001 Kodak Albuquerque International Balloon Fiesta. At this time, all events scheduled for this year's Balloon Fiesta will occur weather permitting. Twenty-one countries will be represented at this year's event. As in years past, we will continue to work with local, state and federal officials to provide a safe venue for our balloonists, spectators, and supporters.

The Balloon Fiesta board of directors, staff, and supporters are deeply saddened by the horrific events that have impacted our country. Our prayers and thoughts are with all of the families affected by the terrorism."

—Press release issued by Tom Garrity, Balloon Fiesta media spokesperson, September 11, 2001

On 9/11—the tragic day the World Trade Center fell and thousands died in New York, at the Pentagon, and aboard Flight 93—the 30th Albuquerque International Balloon Fiesta (AIBF) was less than a month away. All aircraft in the United States were grounded as a precaution against further terrorist hijackings. This, of course, included balloons. For all of the optimism expressed in the Balloon Fiesta's press statement that the event would go forward on schedule, the fate of the event was far from certain. No one knew whether the restrictions on balloon flight would be lifted in time.

In any event, most people had other things on their minds. Nearly everyone seemed to have lost a friend, family member, or business associate in the tragedy, or knew someone who had. This e-mail came from one of my balloon crew:

Balloon Fiesta Mass Ascension, October 7, 2001. At this moment, U.S. troops were beginning thir march info Afghanistan.

Kim, this morning (9/13) I received an e-mail that 38 people from one of the research firms that I communicate with are unaccounted for. Change the number of my friends and associates missing from 72 to 110. Thanks for visit last night. Sorry I was such bad company.

She had not been bad company, of course, though it would have been perfectly understandable if she had. She was to get good news about one of her friends, but alas, not the other 109.

And there was this, from a balloonist friend:

Thank you all for the condolences I have received from all of you…We have received official notice that my cousin perished on September 11 at his job on the 105th floor of the World Trade Center. It just goes to show how we are all affected by this incident, no matter how far we live from it. If I may ask a favor of balloonist worldwide that can. Please fly an American Flag from your crown line once VFR flights are allowed for a former balloonist not able to fly right now…God bless all of you, and God bless the USA.

It was this sort of thinking that, at least in my mind in that climate, made me want to go fly my balloon as a patriotic act. Take that, you dirty rotten scoundrels! But the FAA was proceeding with understandable caution in reopening U.S. airspace. While scheduled commercial air service was back in the air within a few days, general aviation (private aircraft, including balloons) remained grounded. At the Balloon Fiesta offices, Executive Director Paul Smith, Event Director Pat Brake, and members of the Board of Directors were lobbying anybody that had anything to do with federal airspace

limitations. That year, Harry Season was Balloon Fiesta President, and he remembers:

We worked very closely with the NM Congressional delegation to help break logjams. I was on the phone with the FAA Command Post in Washington, DC almost every day providing them information as to what the AIBF event actually consisted of. They kept saying that they understood that we were just balloons, but as ballooning falls in the General Aviation category and all GA was grounded we just had to wait. Of course we were faced with many international pilots who had already shipped their balloons and were desperately trying to get here and we wanted to know if we could hold the event or not. I recall that another balloon event a week earlier than AIBF (in Texas I believe) had to cancel their flights and just did tethers for a few days.

But it was slow going. On Wednesday, September 19, Paul Smith issued this update:

Wed. 9/19: . . . Many of you may know that the FAA imposed a prohibition against flying immediately after the attacks. Since that initial prohibition of all flights, the FAA has allowed different categories of flights to occur after they have been able to examine the importance of the proposed type of flight, the potential risks of the type of flight in light of last week's tragedies and the potential methods to safely perform the flights…Currently the FAA ban still applies to VFR (Visual Flight Rules) general aviation; this includes balloons. New Mexico's congressional delegation has been working on removing the ban from balloon flights. We have received word that this ban may be lifted as early as this week. Thus, we don't anticipate any change to our schedule, however if any changes are made, we will post them immediately to our website…As in past years, we will continue to work with local, state and federal officials to provide a safe venue for our participants, guests, and supporters. We don't plan to discuss our security plans. To do so would lessen their effectiveness. However I can say that plans are being made in conjunction with the appropriate agencies and based on the best information that we receive.

The very next day, the effort paid off: Paul wrote:

VFR flight is again allowed in the United States. In other words, balloons can fly…We are still reviewing the NOTAM (Notice to Airmen) to determine whether there are any provisions that will affect the Balloon Fiesta, but as you can imagine, we are ecstatic about the reinstatement of balloon flights. The Balloon Fiesta, and balloonists in general, are very thankful to the efforts of New Mexico's Congressional delegation and in particular Senator Pete Domenici and Congresswoman Heather Wilson. All the information that

Kim Vesely's balloon with battle colors flying!

we've received indicates that their actions were instrumental in the reinstatement of balloon flights.

This was good news indeed, but the Balloon Fiesta, with its massive crowds, international participation, and cross-country gas balloon race, was a complicated event and some things remained uncertain. Paul's update the next day alluded to some of this:

…Because this whole process is new to everyone, there have been some glitches in restoring general aviation. While Balloon Fiesta will be able to fly under the current rules, parts of Balloon Fiesta would be affected. We are working with the FAA and New Mexico's Congressional delegation to help restore the original rules…On Saturday, October 6th during our Opening Ceremonies, the Balloon Fiesta will pay tribute to the United States and remember the victims of the tragic events that occurred on September 11th. We would like everyone to bring your American Flag and fly it from your balloon in the Mass Ascension. Please pass this message along to any pilots that you know.

The Balloon Fiesta staff had, in fact, gone to some effort to try to acquire flags for pilots to fly from their balloons. But in the wave of patriotism that followed 9/11, American flags were hard to come by. Eventually, someone suggested I visit a local VFW post, so I headed off to Post 5890 in Rio Rancho. The veterans there were very helpful but, like everyone else, had run out of flags. Then, one remembered they had a somewhat faded, battered flag in the back of the post that they'd planned to destroy. He suggested that I fly them as "battle colors," and I was proud to do so.

In this atmosphere, the 30th Balloon Fiesta began. Harry Season writes:

I will never forget my opening speech that morning (a tradition that the AIBF President opens the event with a few words). Just 3 weeks since 9/11, the world still reeling from what had happened and so unsure as to what was going to happen next. I spoke of the camaraderie of ballooning, the Balloon Fiesta being a place that all nationalities could gather in peace, and the beauty of flight itself as a means of lifting one's spirit. That year was certainly my proudest ever both as a member of the AIBF and as an individual accomplishment.

And with that, Balloon Fiesta was off and flying. The FAA had even allowed the America's Challenge Gas Balloon Race, an international cross-country event, to go on as scheduled. Nineteen gas balloons lifted off and headed northeastward across the Great Plains. But if people in Albuquerque were used to and not startled by balloons, this certainly wasn't true in the Midwest. Peter Cuneo, who won the race with Barbara Fricke, recalls landing in a field while a very nervous law enforcement officer eyed them from a nearby road. Peter walked out to meet the lawman, who after some uncomfortable conversation revealed the cause of his nervousness: he'd observed the pilots dropping a brown powder from the basket. As the anthrax scares that followed 9/11 were then big news, it took Peter a small amount of persuading to convince the law officer that they weren't terrorists, had merely been ballasting sand, and that they really would like him to come out to the balloon and endorse their landing certificate.

Cuneo and Fricke weren't the only team that raised suspicions. Harry Season remembers:

After the event started and we got the gas race off, I got a call from the FBI that an aircraft had been spotted somewhere in the upper Midwest (South Dakota maybe?) and appeared to be dropping red liquid from its basket at night, which caused quite a stir in the area. After some investigation through our Gas Command Post we were pretty certain that the gas balloon was Bruce Hale's. I advised the FBI that most likely what was happening was that Bruce was ballasting sand and when seen against the strobing red aircraft warning light probably DID look like liquid. In any case, we were told to have Mr. Hale contact the local Sheriff and FBI immediately upon landing, which he promptly did. This story and many others associated with VERY nervous local, state and Federal Law Enforcement officials who we had assembled into a team and met every morning at the Balloon Fiesta Park to share information about potential threats, made for a most interesting 2001 AIBF.

Balloonists on the field had also been advised to take extra security precautions, which we all duly did. We soon got used to the Black Hawk helicopter orbiting the field; in fact it was kind of nice to see it up there. Then, two days into the event, the U.S. invaded Afghanistan, which ratcheted up the anxiety all over again. For all of that, from the standpoint of someone flying in the event, Balloon Fiesta was surprisingly normal. The weather that year was good and despite fears of mass cancellations most balloonists made it to Albuquerque, along with thousands of spectators.

Yet, things weren't normal. Four of my seven regular crew members had lost friends in New York. Like most people, I felt very helpless in the wake of 9/11. Just about the only thing I could do was throw my balloon in the air, battle colors hanging proudly from the crownline, almost as an act of defiance. It proved to be a catharsis for me and my friends and, I believe, for Albuquerque. As Harry Season had so aptly said, it was truly a lift for the spirit in one of our country's bleakest hours.

❑ Kim Vesely, with Harry Season, Paul Smith, Peter Cuneo, Tom Garrity, and ballooning friends, 2006

Pins, Patches
and Other Daubles of Affection

Since the start of ballooning in 1783, balloonists and observers alike have had their own personal ways of keeping their ballooning memories close at hand. While the most common form of memories are probably photographs, there is a large world of hobby enthusiasts that feverishly collect and treasure balloon pins.

Pins typically range in size from as small as ¼" all the way up to very rare examples checking in at over 8". Pins are traditionally manufactured from some form of metal and a variant of enamel type materials that provide the colors on the pin.

Early pins were primarily metals with very little if any color, varying from bronze to sterling silver or even solid gold. Later, a beautiful type of pin evolved called "cloisonné" which entailed the melting of glass type materials that are common in many types of jewelry. True cloisonné pins are quite expensive to produce and in the 1980's, alternative forms started to appear to help keep the cost down but they also provided a wider, broader scope of colors. Present day pins are limited only by imagination with bright colors, springs, flashing lights and other enhancements being commonplace.

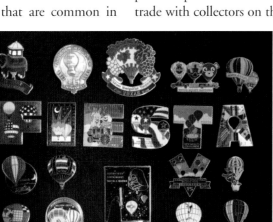

An assortment of pins produced by AIBF and private pilots, some dating back to 1933.

The most common pins are often exact miniature representations of the balloons themselves. Some balloon owners choose to produce several different versions of their pins each year, some for people lucky enough to fly in the balloon, others for crew members and others that they might freely trade, sell or give away, and others that simply represent their balloon. Though not all balloonists produce pins, most that do are usually happy to trade with collectors on the field. The best time to trade with a pilot or crew member is either before inflation or, even better, after their flight is over and the work is done.

The easiest way to obtain a pin or start collecting is by purchasing pins from the Albuquerque International Balloon Fiesta official tents on the field during Balloon Fiesta. Buying two or three provides extras

KOB-TV weatherman Steve Stucker at Balloon Fiesta.

and assist them in completing their collections.

Sure, a picture is worth a thousand words, but just how much is a pin worth? As with anything, value is determined via supply and demand. Traders and collectors will search high and low for the "hot" pin each year at Balloon Fiesta. Those pins vary each year from the obvious (Darth Vader) to the unexpected (official AIBF Pin Trading Day pins). Age is also a factor in value as it is with most collectibles. As time goes by, who knows where people display or put them for safekeeping. The pin that you could find for $1 at seemingly every concessionaire's booth in 1982 might run you $50 today, assuming you can find one at all. Some individual pins today bring more than $300 each based

This pin commemorating the 10th anniversary of the Balloon Fiesta Dawn Patrol Show may just be the largest ever produced. It was commissioned by the participating pilots and weighs more than most belt buckles. The Dawn Patrol group promptly dubbed it "Pin-zilla."

that can be used as "traders."

Most ballooning events also produce "event" pins for the event itself as well as events within the event. At Balloon Fiesta, you'll find many pins each year produced for everything from balloon glows to the zebras acting as Launch Directors on the field. Even the Balloon Fiesta Board Members have personalized pins each year. Balloon Fiesta is in the process of creating an online website database to help collectors determine what has been produced

Some collectors buy or build display boards and cases to show-off their collections.

on scarcity and demand. An average pin will usually cost from five to twenty dollars.

It's a common sight to see vests, hats and jackets covered from top to bottom with people's complete collections, regardless of value or maybe just one or two of their favorites. Locals and visitors alike always look forward to local celebrity newscaster Steve Stucker as he reports live from the field covered head to (nearly) toe with his favorite pins. Some people will happily trade what they proudly display while others would never dream of parting with even one of their many acquisitions. Balloon Fiesta has recently added two "balloon pin trading days" to the event each year so traders can get together and swap pins, tell stories and catch up with friends they may only see once a year, during Balloon Fiesta.

Other forms of collectibles have become popular over the years including patches, posters and trading cards. Trading cards provide a more affordable item for pilots and crews to give away to the growing number of balloon fanatics each year. Since 1979, Balloon Fiesta has produced an official poster for the event and they have become quite collectible in their own right.

The true value associated with a particular pin or collectible should always be the great memories it brings back every time you see it, wherever that might be.

❏ Ty Young, 2010

The Dream Lives On

Albuquerque not only celebrates 40 years of hosting the Albuquerque International Balloon Fiesta, but it also celebrates three generations of balloonists. Many grown up children of our earliest balloon pilots have become balloonists themselves, and in turn many of them have raised their children to become balloonists. As in generations past, today's younger set dreams of flying in a balloon and these dreams do come true. It is the launching of these great dreams and seeing them take flight that brings out the kid in everyone, and propels the Balloon Fiesta into the future.

But it is not just this local propagation of balloonists that keeps the magic alive - it is our endless community spirit, excellent flying conditions, wide open spaces, festival atmosphere and undying camaraderie that bring pilots and fans back year after year—a growing family that embraces you for a lifetime. It is the photographer's paradise, a kaleidescope of vibrant colors and shapes painted on the vast canvas of Albuquerque's famous blue sky —the most photographed event in the history of mankind. It is walking a meandering path among swaying giants as the sun squints over the Sandias. It is losing yourself in a field of color, as if one were inside a giant bubble machine. It is a lucky encounter with a pilot and instant recruitment to lend a hand with inflation. It is igniting a raging fire in burners and in the hearts of prospective first-time flyers. It is climbing into the basket on the threshold of an adventure and letting that balloon sweep you off your feet and lift you above the crowd. It is an unparalleled ride that dares to exceed anything you can conjure up in your finest fantasy.

It is amazing how far we have come through the past four decades. It has been an awesome journey, from 13 balloons lifting off from a shopping center to the most colorful aerial extravaganza staged anywhere on the planet. With splashes of living color in high-definition and the roar of burners in surround-sound, Balloon Fiesta Park becomes the production studio on a grand scale. And this amazing show will definitely go on.

And that show is not just balloons. It is also the famous breakfast burritos on Main Street, the herd of zebras orchestrating orderly mass ascensions, and chase crews scrambling to catch up to their balloon. It is also the peripheral events that are integral to the Balloon Fiesta—parades, ceremonies, stunt flyers, fireworks, concerts, art shows, craft fairs, kite-flying, zoo parties and gala dinners. And finally, it is that special season in New Mexico, with the smell of chiles roasting and pinon firewood burning, quaking aspens turning mountainsides into aprons of gold, sun-painted valley cottonwoods, honking Canada geese heading south in the Rio Grande flyway, red chile ristras hanging in doorways, the crisp October air—all helping to set the stage for the Balloon Fiesta. Autumn in New Mexico – that's when the state shows her true colors and the Bal-

175

loon Fiesta captures the sights, sounds and smells of this very special time of year.

Albuquerque will forever be known as the Balloon Capital of the World. With its dazzling trademark events—Dawn Patrol, Flight of the Nations, Special Shapes Rodeo and Balloon Glow—as well as innovative flying events, it has earned its place as the most famous destination for sport ballooning. Visitors from all over the United States and across the globe will always be welcome in our friendly skies.

Albuquerque's unbridled passion for flight without wings is the stuff that will keep the Balloon Fiesta going. Its ability to supply a huge army of volunteers each year will guarantee continued success. Vigorous public support, a growing team of loyal sponsors, and homegrown leadership will sustain the Balloon Fiesta to its golden anniversary and beyond. The event is matchless, the opportunities boundless.

What lies ahead for the Albuquerque International Balloon Fiesta is yet to be uncovered, for all we really can do is look at our proud heritage—where we have been, what we have done. With each Balloon Fiesta being a bright, shiny link in a continuous chain of fiestas, we can only imagine what the Balloon Fiesta will be like for future generations. It is our young people who will frolic in the future, and like us, will reach out from a balloon basket and try to touch the sky. And perhaps along the way, they will finally see the peace of ballooning transcend all nations so that we can all live more tranquil lives.

The Albuquerque International Balloon Fiesta is where adventures begin and memories never end.

❏ Dick Brown, 2011

Afterword

How can one find words to describe being a thousand feet in the air on a cool New Mexico morning, standing in a open wicker car, seeing beyond the horizon, held up by nothing more than heated air and nylon? How do you say you have made the dearest of lifelong friends and learned extraordinary things at a hot-air balloon rally at a southwestern cattle ranch? How to picture grown men and women in outrageous costumes, with kids in tow, having more fun than anyone ever imagined? How do you portray something that has changed your life, and convince others that it's true? I offer my simple verse, written in 1992, dedicated to my family, my friends and myself:

Ode to Ballooning (Two Friends)
[with apologies to Harry Chapin]

Don and I, we went ballooning
We were gonna learn to fly;
He took off to find the moment
I took off to find the sky.

He had the touch, he had the feel
I had the tenacity to try;
He took off and found the moment
I took off and found the sky.

The editors have been writing about ballooning and the Albuquerque International Balloon Fiesta for more than 35 years apiece: a fair feat since none of us freely admits to being that old. For each of us, writing and editing this material was a journey through 39 years of wonderful memories. We hope you have enjoyed the trip as much as we have.

❏ Tom McConnell, 2011

Authors/Contributors

Dick Brown

While a former submariner and balloonist, Dick Brown has still managed to keep his feet on dry land as a 44-year resident of New Mexico. He has been a licensed commercial balloon pilot since 1973 and was most active in ballooning when he owned an AX-7 and flew in the early Balloon Fiestas. For several years he was the Editor of AAAA's *Cloudbouncer* newsletter and during the period 1974-1979 he was the Editor of the BFA's *Ballooning Journal*. He also wrote a "how-to" book on Hot Air Ballooning which was published in 1978 and he produced a monthly newsletter for a major balloon manufacturer for 17 years. He was awarded the BFA's President's Service Award in 1976 and he and his wife, Donna, received the BFA's Shields-Trauger Memorial Award in 1979 for exemplary service. He was the recipient of AAAA's 1979 Sid Cutter Traveling Trophy and the FAI's 1980 Montgolfier Diploma for service to the sport of ballooning. He still keeps his hand in ballooning as a Balloon Fiesta volunteer and member of AIBF's Heritage Committee where each year he writes feature articles for the Official Fiesta Program.

Sid Cutter

Sid Cutter is a life-long native of Albuquerque and an Air Force veteran. Legend has it that he was born with flying in his blood. He has been a licensed balloon pilot since 1962, long before he even saw his first modern hot air balloon. While still operating Cutter Flying Service in 1971, he purchased one of Albuquerque's first hot air balloons, founded the Albuquerque Aerostat As-cension Association (AAAA) and became a distributor for a major balloon manufacturer. He flew the Roadrunner balloon in the "First Albuquerque Balloon Fiesta" and served as Balloonmeister for the 1973, 1974 and 1975 Balloon Fiestas. Sid organized the first two World Hot Air Balloon Championships and was awarded the FAI's 1975 Montgolfier Diploma for service to the sport of ballooning. Sid's hard work and devotion led directly to the creation of the non-profit organization known as Albuquerque International Balloon Fiesta, Inc. The AAAA honored Albuquerque's "Father of Ballooning" with the annual Sid Cutter Traveling Trophy, which it awards annually in his name to recognize service to the sport. In 1978, he won the U.S. National Hot Air Balloon Championships. Perhaps long overdue, in 1983, in gratitude for his numerous contributions to ballooning in Albuquerque, Sid was inducted into the Balloon Fiesta Hall of Fame. In 1986, he again won the Nationals and to this day remains active in ballooning, a legend in his own time. Sid is the real reason Albuquerque is known as the Balloon Capital of the World.

John Davis

John Davis, one of Albuquerque's ballooning pioneers, began flying balloons in 1973 and for much of his life has promoted balloon safety and competitive flying. He also holds the longevity record for service on the Balloon Fiesta Board: more than 30 years; he served as president in 1982 and Balloonmeister in 1988 and 1989. For many years, John was an FAA Safety Counselor and FAA Designated Examiner, and has officiated at numerous balloon competitions around the world including the U.S. National Championships. John is the recipient of the AAAA Sid Cutter Award (1982), BFA Shields-Trauger Award (2004) Elizabeth J. Dumont Safety Award (1998), and FAA Accident Prevention Counselor of the Year (1984). He acted as project director for several world record-setting flights made by his wife, the late renowned balloonist Carol Rymer Davis, in the late 1970's and early 1980's. John is the current chair of the AIBF Heritage Committee.

Tom McConnell

A pathologist and pioneer faculty member of the University of New Mexico School of Medicine, Dr. Tom McConnell originally came to Albuquerque to serve a rotating internship at the old Bernalillo County-Indian Hospital in 1962-63. He never left, next serving a residency in pathology at the hospital and the infant University of New Mexico School of Medicine, then joining the faculty later in 1967. He was Chief of the Pathology Service and Director of the Cytogenetics Section at UNM Hospital at the time of his retirement in 1998. Tom is one of Albuquerque's earliest and most visible balloon pilots, part of the second "class" of balloon pilots trained through the Albuquerque Aerostat Ascension Association (AAAA) in 1973. His family's *Zia* balloon, in the pattern of the New Mexico state flag, has become a widely-recognized symbol of the Land of Enchantment. Tom became the second President of AAAA in 1974 and is the 1987 recipient of the AAAA Sid Cutter Award for service to ballooning. He has served on the Albuquerque International Balloon Fiesta Board of Directors since 1979, was President of the Board in 1992, and was elected to the Balloon Fiesta Hall of Fame in 1995. Dr. McConnell is one of the leading experts in the country on balloon accident forensics, having written several articles and a book on the subject. He conducts balloon safety seminars at events throughout the country. Over the past 35 years, wife Mary and family have extended their hospitality to dozens of dignitaries,

politicians, celebrities, and just plain folks from all over the world visiting the Balloon Fiesta.

Paul Rhetts

Paul got his first exposure to Fiesta-fever back in 1984 while visiting Albuquerque for a friend's wedding. Even now after more than 20 years working on a balloon crew on the *After Midnight* and *Sunflyer* balloons, the excitement is still there. Paul has also been in the book publishing business for over 34 years, the last 20 as the co-owner of LPD Press & Rio Grande Books. He served as the principal designer and publisher for this book.

Kim Vesely

As a former TV news reporter and freelance writer, Kim Vesely has been writing about balloonists and ballooning for more than 30 years. She became involved in ballooning as a reporter and producer for KOB-TV, covering the Balloon Fiesta and many of ballooning's great "firsts" including the Double Eagle II trans-Atlantic crossing, Double Eagle V trans-Pacific crossing, and the Kitty Hawk flight across North America. In December 1979, Kim was one of the co-organizers of the first Luminaria Tour Balloon Display, often recognized as the world's first organized "balloon glow". She is the 1992 recipient of the Sid Cutter Award for service to ballooning and the 2009 recipient of the Balloon Fiesta Heritage Award. Kim served on the Balloon Fiesta Board (1988-89), the AAAA Board (1982-83), the AIBF Heritage Committee (1999-present), and the Board of Trustees for the Anderson-Abruzzo Albuquerque International Balloon Museum (2003-11). Kim has been an active Balloon Fiesta volunteer since 1979 and since 2002 has been the volunteer editor of the Balloon Fiesta program and the America's Challenge Command Center media liaison; additionally, her articles on ballooning have appeared in Ballooning, Balloon Life, and other publications. Professionally, for the last ten years Kim has served as Communications Officer for Rio Rancho

Public Schools. Kim is a hot-air balloon pilot; her late husband Bob and stepson Scott are also balloonists and longtime participants in the Balloon Fiesta.

Karen Yoor

Denverite Karen Yoor, a travel writer, publishes in numerous newspapers in the United States and Canada, and writes articles on a variety of subjects. By far, her favorite theme is hot air ballooning and within that category, special shapes provide the best material. She has ground crewed for *Balloon Hilda*, the witch; *Big Foot*, an enormous sneaker; and *Arky*, a sort of zoo on a flying boat. She thanks The Canadian Tourism group for allowing her to fulfill her obsession to fly in a special shape balloon by allowing her spirit to soar in both the *Maple Leaf* balloon and *Mountie*, the larger than life Canadian cop astride a horse. She credits Pilot Doug Taggart from California for her interest in all areas of ballooning. He suggested many facets of the sport which she covered in articles for the Albuquerque International Balloon Fiesta's official program, including stories on Crewing (Frequent Flier Smiles), Dawn Patrol (Early Risers), Propane (Fuel of Fun), Launch officials (Zebras have Zits), The Balloon Quilt (The Great Cover Up) and other lofty subjects, which gave her the opportunity to work with many different pilots and Fiesta officials. Jodi Baugh, her friend and former AIBF Media Chief and program editor, got Karen involved more than a decade ago.

Ty Young

Ty Young began collecting balloon pins and other memorabilia when he was 6 years old, disappearing for hours on end within the safe confines of the Balloon Fiesta's old Simms Field, trading pins and hanging out with the pilots of the world. Ty's balloon pin collection slowly and unexpectedly turned from a nice hobby into an obsession, and is now believed to be the largest in the world at well over 30,000 pins. Ty is currently in the process of adding an official pin reference guide to the Balloon Fiesta website as a resource for balloon aficionados and collectors around the world. He currently sits on the AIBF Board of Directors and continues to use his 1941 American LaFrance fire truck chase vehicle each year at the Balloon Fiesta. Professionally, Ty is managing partner of Young Equity Partners, a real estate holding company, and a former restaurateur and financial advisor.

AIBF Heritage Committee

John C. Davis IV, Chair
Dick Brown
Sid Cutter
Gary Dewey
Jacqueline Hockey
Charlotte Kinney
Rod May
Tom McConnell, M.D.
Pat Murphy
Paul Rhetts
Dick Rice
Tom Rutherford
Harry Season
John Sena
Jim Shiver
Jeffrey Cooper-Smith
Mark Sullivan
Kim Vesely
Ty Young

Acknowledgements/Photo Credits

In 1970, if anybody had ventured that an event featuring hot air balloons would be the biggest annual event in New Mexico and one of the truly great national (international!) events in the United States, the city fathers of Albuquerque would have rightly said, "You're nuts!" Fortunately for all of us, Sid Cutter was nuts enough to say "Yes!" to KOB's request that he bring his balloon to their 50th anniversary gala—and then crazy enough to think of bringing in a bunch of other balloonists (to which KOB was crazy enough to say, "Yes!"). Former Albuquerque Mayor Harry Kinney and many others kept the dream alive; and thousands of volunteers and professionals perpetuated it with a love that shines through with every mass ascension. We thank them and all of the sponsors and concessionaires whose support has been so vital through the years.

Every year there has been a Balloon Fiesta, there has been a Balloon Fiesta official program. The first was eight mimeographed (remember mimeographing?) pages. But from the second year (1973) on, the program has chronicled the balloons, pilots, and an ever-changing palette of activities. The editors of this book owe a debt of gratitude to the people—mostly uncredited—who have been responsible for the compilation and production of the program. Because much of their work was uncredited, it was difficult for us to identify all of them. Key figures we could track include Sid Cutter, Kathy Hart, Aubrey Cookman, Ron Behrmann, Jean Jordan, Marjorie Shapiro Stein, and Jodi Baugh. If we missed anyone, we apologize and thank you. Dozens of writers have contributed material to Balloon Fiesta programs. We wish we could have included every article, but couldn't without making this volume the size of the Bronx phone book. Maybe someday …

We also want to acknowledge the help of Marilee Schmitt-Nason of the Anderson-Abruzzo Albuquerque International Balloon Museum for her help in securing photographs from the museum archives. Personally, we all owe a debt of gratitude to our ballooning mentors whose willingness to share the sport with us has so enriched our lives. As Kim Vesely has said, "We came for the ballooning, and stayed for the people." This sport has brought all of us friendships that last a lifetime. We are also grateful to our families and friends for putting up with the ballooning craziness.

All photographs are copyright of the photographer and are used here with permission.

Source Material & Selected Resouces

BOOKS:

Aeronauts, Aerostats and Aerosataion: Sport, Pastime, and Adventure Ballooning in the American West, Robert Knight Barney, Journal of the West, Vol. 22, No. 1, January 1983

Albuquerque: Where the World Celebrates Ballooning, Steve Young, Kim Vesely, and Marjorie Shapiro Stein, Q13-KRQE TV and American and World Geographic Publishing, 1996

Around the World in 20 Days, Bertrand Piccard and Brian Jones, John Wiley and Sons, Inc. 1999 (published in Britain as *The Greatest Adventure: The Round-The-World Balloon Voyage of the Breitling Orbiter 3*)

Balloon Pins: The Definitive Reference, Frank Prell, Oxford Promotions, Ltd., 1985

Ballooning: The Complete Guide to Riding the Winds, Dick Wirth and Jerry Young, Random House, 1980

Balloons Are for Chasing, Calvin Campbell, Zia Enterprises, 1985

Balloon Safety Seminars, Thomas S. McConnell, MD, Rio Grande Books, 2009

The Book of Balloons, Erik Norgaard, Crown Publishers, 1971

Chasing the Wind: The Autobiography of Steve Fossett, Virgin Books, Ltd., 2006

Come Up and Get Me: An Autobiography of Colonel Joe Kittinger, Joe Kittinger and Craig Ryan, University of New Mexico Press, 2010

Double Eagle: Ben Abruzzo, Maxie Anderson, and Larry Newman, Charles McCarry, Little Brown and Company, 1979

Fiesta Memories, Patrick Lee and Peter W. Richardson, Balloon Passion Communication, 1994

Flight of the Pacific Eagle: Ben Abruzzo, Larry Newman, Ron Clark, and Rocky Aoki, Ray Nelson, Adobe Press, Inc., 1985

The Grand Challenge: New Mexico and its Influence on Ballooning, Anderson Abruzzo Albuquerque International Balloon Museum, 2004

The Great Balloon Festival, Ed Dosien and Joe Nigg, Free Flight Press, Inc., 1989

Hot Air Ballooning, Dick Brown, TAB Books, 1979

Hot Air Balloons, Christine Kalakuka and Brent Stockwell, Friedman/Fairfax, 1998

The Joy of Ballooning, George Denniston, Courage Books, 1999

The Pre-Astronauts: Manned Ballooning on the Threshold of Space, Craig Ryan, Naval Institute Press, 1995

Ride the Wind USA To Africa: Richard Abruzzo, Troy Bradley, Anne Hillerman, Rio Grande Publishing, 1995

Riding the Jetstream: The Story of Ballooning from Montgolfier to Breitling, John Christopher, John Murray Publishers, 2001

The Romance of Ballooning, Edita Lausanne, Viking Press, 1971

PERIODICALS:

Albuquerque International Balloon Fiesta Official Programs, 1972-2010

Ballooning, the journal of the Balloon Federation of America, 1968-present

Balloon Life Magazine, published 1986-2006

Aerostat Magazine, the official journal of the British Balloon and Airship Club

Cloudbouncer, Albuquerque Aerostat Ascension Association monthly newsletter, 1973-present

SELECTED ONLINE RESOURCES:

www.balloonfiesta.com Albuquerque International Balloon Fiesta Official Web Site

www.hotairballooning.org Albuquerque Aerostat Ascension Association Web site

www.bfa.org Balloon Federation of America Web site

www.fai.org Fédération Aéronautique Internationale, the international sanctioning body for all air sports, including ballooning. Tons of great information on world record flights, the Coupe Gordon Bennett, and more!

www.naa.aero National Aeronautic Association, the U.S. sanctioning body for air sports.

www.gasballooning.net Brian Critelli's site about all things gas ballooning

www.ballooning.org/ballooning/balloon-media.html Good listing of ballooning books and periodicals